The Australian Country Kitchen

Edited by HELEN VELLACOTT

The Australian Country Kitchen

*A book of fine old recipes
for contemporary cooks*

VIKING

Viking

Penguin Books Australia Ltd

487 Maroondah Highway, PO Box 257

Ringwood, Victoria 3134, Australia

Penguin Books Ltd

Harmondsworth, Middlesex, England

Viking Penguin, A Division of Penguin Books USA Inc.

375 Hudson Street, New York, New York 10014, USA

Penguin Books Canada Limited

10 Alcorn Avenue, Toronto, Ontario, Canada M4V 3B2

Penguin Books (N.Z.) Ltd

182–190 Wairau Road, Auckland 10, New Zealand

First published by Penguin Books Australia Ltd 1995

10 9 8 7 6 5 4 3 2 1

Copyright © Penguin Books Australia, 1995

Compiled by Sarah Dawson

Designed by Guy Mirabella

Photography and styling by Simon Griffiths

Typeset in New Baskerville Roman by Bookset, Melbourne

Printed by Kyodo Printing Co., Singapore

National Library of Australia
Cataloguing-in-Publication data

The Australian country kitchen: a book of fine old
recipes for contemporary cooks.

   Bibliography.
   Includes index.
   ISBN 0 670 90639 5.

   1. Cookery, Australian. 2. Cookery, Australian – History.
   I. Vellacott, Helen, 1911–

641.5994

Servings: All the recipes in this book serve 4–6 people.

CONTENTS

ℐNTRODUCTION

A Kitchen Harvest

THE RECIPES IN THIS BOOK have been garnered from the many Australian cookery manuals published in the nineteenth and early twentieth centuries – those far-off times when housewives or their cooks, in hot, steamy kitchens, managed to produce, day after day, a remarkable volume and variety of food. In these books we glimpse hearty meat breakfasts, even heartier midday dinners, and dainty afternoon teas that helped women of leisure to while away the hours. We can almost hear, too, the crackle of the starched white cloths spread for the evening meal and the rustle of flowers and fruit in elaborate epergnes, and catch the glimmer of the silver and cut-crystal on the sideboard.

The enormous influence of Australia's early cookery books is reflected in the fact that some ran to fifty editions, with sales reaching hundreds of thousands – at a time when Australia's population was a fraction of its present size. The first of these, *English and Australian Cookery*, was written in Tasmania in 1864. It was a leather-bound volume by Edward Abbott, a member of parliament, who enjoyed good living. Each state came to have its own favourite recipe book, which listed dishes that were specially suited to its particular climate and conditions.

The flood of local cookery books came in answer to the frustration felt by housewives here when they turned for help to books published in 'the old country'. The young Mrs Lance Rawson put the matter in a nutshell in her first book, published in the 1870s, when she said, 'Almost every young matron has among her wedding presents a good Cookery Book, either Mrs Beeton, Warne, or some other equally good and useful for town use, but which, in the bush, owing to the scant material to work with, becomes nearly useless.' In fact, many of the cookery books that housewives consulted in colonial days were far older than Mrs Beeton's: they were the hand-written kitchen notebooks of their mothers, or even their grandmothers, that had been added to, in differing scripts and spellings, over the years and contained a wide variety of recipes, cures and

GENERAL OBSERVATIONS ON AUSTRALIAN COOKERY

COOKERY IN AUSTRALIA is to all intents and purposes English. The dishes are the same, the mode is the same, and the order of serving meals precisely what it is in England. An Englishman in a good hotel in Sydney or Melbourne would find no difference between that and one of comparative standing at home, except in the matter of expense, the same meals being served in Australia at two-thirds the cost. Were he, however, to penetrate to the region of the chef, he would find that in many hotels, in place of Frenchmen, Chinamen would be the cooks, good cooks of that nationality being found more easily than Frenchmen, so many Chinamen emigrating.

It is well known what marvellous patience Chinamen have, and they bring this quality to bear not only upon the way they cook, but in labour and pains they take to grow provisions, and it is a recognised fact that they are the best gardeners in the Colony, their mode of irrigation being superior to any other.

WAGES IN AUSTRALIA are the only things that render housekeeping in any way as expensive as at home; for it may be reckoned that the pay of female servants is quite doubled when they emigrate. A good cook can easily command from £40 to £50 a year, and in many households a man and wife are engaged in the capacities of butler and cook at excellent salaries. Up country really good servants are very hard to find, and the Australian housewife (no matter to what rank she belongs) ought to be prepared to undertake the duties of any absent domestic, so that a knowledge of cooking and ordinary household work, are necessary qualifications for a settler's wife.

Mrs Beeton's Book of Household Management, 1865

advice on household management. My oldest manuscript cookery book is inscribed, inside the cover, 'Marg¹ Hanmer, September ye 22, 1780'. As in most such volumes the great majority of its recipes are for beverages, and next in number are remedies for all the ills of mankind, and even for the ills of cattle, sheep and dogs. This book was carried out to New Zealand by young William Hanmer on the *Castle Eden* in 1850. His sojourn there was short, for he soon married and took his bride and his cookery book to Old Talgai on Queensland's Darling Downs. Another volume, taken even further north to the tropics, starts off with the date 1842, and not only gives little poems and recipes for delicacies like Pickled Radish Pods and Cucumber Ketchup but even the family's weights – 'Father 9 stone 7, Mother 12 stone 3, down to young John, 4 stone'.

These older books were all alike in assuming that conditions here would be the same as those in England; but who would have had sufficient equipment in her Australian kitchen to make Mrs Raffald's famous Solomon's Temple in Flummery or her Portable Soup for Travellers, useful though the latter would have been on long journeys in the bush? The Portable Soup was made by boiling up three large legs of veal, a leg of beef and a large ham with anchovies and vegetables, until the mixture set as a stiff jelly and could be dried in the sun into flat cakes. Its keeping qualities were put beyond dispute when a quantity of it, made in 1771, was found in an English larder this century and was declared by food authorities to be quite wholesome! In most English cookery books the only mention of Australia was in their instructions for using our tinned and frozen meat. The British had long been familiar with frozen food, for many country mansions had underground ice-houses to provide food out of season; in the early nineteenth century an Oxford don, William Buckland, announced at the conclusion of a dinner party, 'Dear friends, you have just eaten meat one hundred thousand years old' – from a mammoth found frozen in the Siberian ice.

Although Edward Abbott's book included 'Australian' in the title, the dishes in it were almost identical to those served in England. Admittedly he gave instructions for cooking local fish, and suggestions for a few colonial dishes such as Kangaroo Steamer and roasts of black swan or 'Emeu', but most of his recipes were for far grander meals; there was nothing to help the desperate bush housewife who might turn to his book for help in spinning out the last small piece of beef, or to find a dish to tempt a feverish child from the household's meagre stores out of season.

Mrs Rawson realised the shortcomings of such works and wrote, in the preface to her first book, 'One often hears people in the bush complain of the poor living: many say "What can one make of salt beef?" And when I tell my friends that we eat bandicoots, kangaroo rats, wallaby and paddymelon, they look astonished.' Her books did provide recipes for an amazing number of new dishes, but they also gave advice about coping with heat and flies and mosquitoes, and suggested many ways to lessen the housewife's load. So great was her influence that in all the books that followed we can detect a distinct Australian flavour, however much their writers might have been pining for the well-equipped kitchens and all the other niceties of 'home'. Despite the assertion in an Australian edition of *Mrs Beeton's Cookery Book* that appeared at this time, that 'Cookery in Australia is to all intents and purposes English', Australians were at last beginning to accept and adapt to their altered circumstances in the new country and to realise that food could be enjoyable even when it did not conform to the traditional notion of a 'proper' meal.

One of the most influential books in promoting a fresh approach towards all meals was by Dr Philip Muskett, a man who took a completely different stand from Edward Abbott. Born in Melbourne and having gone to Edinburgh to study medicine, Muskett had experience of living in both northern and southern latitudes, and he quickly realised that the diet of most Australians – based as it was on large meat dishes and solid puddings – was more suited to the cold weather of the Old World than to the Mediterranean-type climate that we enjoy here. In *The Art of Living in Australia* (1893) he urged Australians to eat more of their abundant fruit and vegetables, and to lead a more relaxed outdoor life. But his was a lone voice in the wilderness, and it has taken us nearly a century to come to favour the barbecues, the salads and the fruit drinks that he so warmly advocated.

Around the turn of the century a stream of new books appeared, both their titles and their contents reflecting the excitement of the age, with the Commonwealth celebrations bringing royal visitors in the persons of the Duke and Duchess of York – the future George V and Queen Mary, the latter famous for her toques and long-handled umbrellas. Thus the new books bore patriotic titles such as the *Kookaburra Cookery Book*, *The Golden Wattle Cookery Book* and *The Green and Gold Cookery Book* and they had the advantage of being written by women who were only too familiar with the shortcomings of the average Australian kitchen – its inefficient stores, poor lighting and ventilation, and complete lack of refrigeration. These books fall into three main categories: books for the rapidly growing number of prosperous city-dwellers; books, usually by teachers, trying to assist overworked housewives; and books written to popularise new approaches to food, such as vegetarianism.

The most successful book in the first class was probably the *Berrambool Recipe Book*, which was compiled in the rich Western District of Victoria. The prestige of its various contributors is shown by the fact that all the recipes were printed under the name of the hostess who recommended them, rather than under the subject they dealt with (Soups, Meat, and so on). Thus one page, headed by the name of a well-known station owner, gives us recipes for Tomato Toast, Coffee Rolls, Scalloped Salmon, Brandy Cocktail and Sherry Swiggle! Other contributors gave us equally bizarre collections, the editor assuring readers that all the recipes in the book (1400 in total) were used and recommended by its distinguished contributors. No doubt many people were delighted to think that they and their guests could now enjoy exactly the same dishes as the ones that were served at the glittering parties described each day in the social columns of the press. The menu on page 7, like most menus of the time, contained a smattering of French terms: young women seeking the post of governess were always asked, 'Can you teach French with the correct accent?', for every mother wanted her daughter to become an accomplished hostess quite at home with the French names for dishes, which were much used to impress guests. Agnes Stokes, an English girl who worked as a kitchen maid at Melbourne's Government House in the 1880s, infuriated a succession of French chefs by referring to the hors d'oeuvres as 'the how d'you dos'.

Among the books that were written to show people how to improve their diet, however slender their means might be, the most successful were probably those by Mrs Wickham. A cookery teacher with the highest qualifications, she had set out the recipes in Dr Muskett's books on food reform, and her own book, *The Kingswood Cookery Book*, was written to show housewives 'how to vary their means so as to give an additional charm to home life'. Her book certainly offered a very wide variety of dishes, from Rolled Calf's Head and Fried Ox Foot to Irish Stew with Oysters. Other teachers whose books had a wide influence were Miss Drake; Miss Fowler, who was head of domestic science in both Western Australia and South Australia; and Miss Emily Futter in Brisbane.

When gas began to replace the often unreliable wood-burning stoves, numerous cookery books appeared, which gave not only interesting recipes but also the cooking times appropriate for a gas stove. Everyone agreed that gas would lighten the housewife's load and, as one book announced, it meant 'saying goodbye to the old way of cooking with its flushed faces, spoilt tempers, spoilt dinners, discontented servants, distressed mistresses and angry masters'. The Hobart Gas Company issued the *Household Gas Cookery Book*, but one suspects that the bulk of its contents was lifted wholesale from an English book: how else can we explain the 'Food in Season and What to Buy' column for January, which listed pheasants, woodcock, teal, ptarmigan, snipe, partridges and grouse; and the fruit column for July, which listed cherries, currants, damsons, nectarines, raspberries and greengages? The illustrations in this book must surely have come from overseas, too, for the 'Expert Demonstrator' explaining the working of the new stove wears a skirt that sweeps the floor, and an elaborate hat with feathers, and points with shiny kid gloves to the spot where the gas should be lit.

Other books showed how easy the improved kerosene ovens were to use, and others again showed how fuel costs could be reduced by turning to hay-box cookery. By this method a pot of porridge, for instance, was brought to the boil on the stove while the family's evening meal was being cooked, then the lid was put on, the pot plunged into a wooden box tightly packed with hay, and a padded wooden lid dropped down. Lo and behold, by next morning the porridge was perfectly cooked, however early the family might need breakfast. During the First World War, when so many women went out to work, the hay-box was often used to cook a stew for the evening meal.

The fact that vegetarian meals became so popular in Australia is surprising, for meat had long been the staple diet here, appearing at every meal. The earliest books on the subject did not use the word 'vegetarian', but spoke vaguely of 'healthful cookery'. One of the earliest of these was Mrs Colcord's *A Friend in the Kitchen*, published in Melbourne, and its popularity is shown by the fact that my copy, dated 1915, is marked 'Sixteenth Edition – one hundred and fifteen thousand'. Its preface concluded with the wish 'that it may prove a blessing to thousands in many lands'. It not only stressed the importance of good cooking, but introduced readers to new foods such as sweetcorn, and granose biscuits, and entertained them with drawings, jokes and proverbs.

The Women's Christian Temperance Union also set out to reform the eating habits

DISHES SUITABLE FOR A WEDDING RECEPTION

Consommé and Oyster Soup in Cups.

Sandwiches of Fish, Poultry, Meat, Game and Potted Meats,

spread with Mayonnaise, Salad Dressing,

Lettuce, Watercress, and various condiments.

PATTIES

Oyster, Lobster, Prawn, Chicken.

Raised Pies of Veal and Ham and Pork.

SALADS

Lobster and Chicken.

Aspic Jelly, small moulds, with Eggs, Chicken, and Pâté de Foie Gras.

SAVOURIES

Stuffed Olives, Devilled Almonds, Cheese.

Moussé of Chicken.

SWEETS

Jellies and Creams, various, in small moulds.

COLD PUDDINGS

Apricot, Cabinet, and Diplomatic.

CREAMS

Coffee, Apricot, Passion Fruit.

GÂTEAUX AND CAKES

Apricot, Passion Fruit, Moussé Sucré.

Queen, Orange, Cream, Angel, Strawberry,

Coffee, Angelica, Vanilla.

ICES

Vanilla, Strawberry.

BEVERAGES

Tea, Coffee, Chocolate, Ærated Waters,

Claret Cup, Madeira Cup, Chili Wine.

The Kingswood Cookery Book, n.d.

of Australians. Its books had a huge circulation, and the number of firms that advertised in them shows how wide the group's influence was. These books set out recipes for all the popular dishes of the day and included a large section devoted to instructions for making drinks – hot and cold, from fruit, barley and many other ingredients, but all completely free of alcohol.

This cavalcade of cookery books, large ones, small ones, expensive ones and 'sixpenny' ones, provides an intriguing picture of the food our ancestors enjoyed and of the changes that have occurred in what we eat, the way we cook it and the hours at which we sit down to enjoy it. While many old recipes seem bland and heavy by today's standards, there are many more that still have universal appeal and these are set down, with minimal revision, in the pages that follow. Others are reproduced verbatim for their historical or whimsical interest.

> We may live without poetry, music and art;
> We may live without conscience, and live without heart;
> We may live without friends; we may live without books;
> But civilised man cannot live without cooks.

Breakfasts and Brunches

OVER THE YEARS, breakfast has probably changed more than any other meal. How long does it take to prepare today? Two minutes, or perhaps five – usually no longer than is needed to bring out the cereal, bread, milk and juice. How different was breakfast in the past, for here – as with other meals – Australians clung to the habits of 'the Old Country'. As Edward Abbott commented in 1864:

> The housekeeper or mistress of the establishment has an infinite variety to choose from. Meats – cold, of different kinds – poultry, pies, ham, tongue, and game. Hot fish, and broiled chops and steaks, eggs and bacon, omelettes, poached and boiled eggs, toast, muffins, marmalade, butter, jams, and honey, not omitting delicious cakes, made on a girdle from Jones's patent flour, which, buttered hot, are light, wholesome, and nutritious. Tea, coffee, and fruits assorted.

He gave many recipes for breakfast dishes, some for city people, some for those roughing it in the bush who, if their digestive systems were strong enough, might be tempted to start the day with Pan Jam: kangaroo tails roasted, skinned and jointed, then fried in a pan with mushrooms – 'first rate tack'. Even more daunting was Slippery Bob, which consisted of kangaroo brains mixed with flour and fried in deep fat.

Even a half-century later, cookery books still included pages of suggestions for breakfasts, many of which seem incredible today: hashed mutton, blade steak, curried eggs, beef rissoles, potted meat, kidney savoury . . . Some of these dishes obviously entailed hours of preparation, and we are left wondering at what unearthly hour the housewife or the cook had to rise in order to produce them. Yet some of the lighter and simpler dishes are ideal for a leisurely breakfast or brunch.

HOT EGG NOG
Beat an egg and place it in a tumbler with a little sugar and a liqueur-glass of rum or brandy. Stir well, then fill the tumbler with hot milk and grate a little nutmeg over the top.

Pancakes from Cardiff

6 tablespoons flour
2 tablespoons sugar
3 tablespoons sour cream
pinch of salt
3 eggs

$^{1}/_{2}$ teaspoon bicarbonate of
  soda
1 tablespoon cream of tartar
1–2 tablespoons water
$^{1}/_{2}$ cup milk

Beat together the flour, sugar, sour cream, salt and eggs. Combine the bicarbonate of soda with the cream of tartar and add to the batter. Gradually add milk until the mixture is bubbly but not too thick. Grease a pan lightly and then pour in mixture, tilting pan slightly until batter spreads. Turn pancake when surface becomes lacy. Serve simply spread with butter, or with lemon juice, sugar and a scattering of finely chopped lemon peel.

Buckwheat Pancakes

$^{1}/_{2}$ cup buckwheat flour
$^{1}/_{2}$ cup plain flour
2 teaspoons baking powder
2 tablespoons sugar

pinch of salt
1 egg
2 tablespoons melted butter
$^{1}/_{2}$ cup milk

Sift together the flours, baking powder, sugar and salt. Beat in the egg and butter, mixing well, and then add enough of the milk to make a creamy batter. Grease a heavy-based frying pan and bring to a medium heat. Pour in 2 tablespoons of the batter and cook until the top is bubbly and the base is golden-brown. Turn with a spatula and brown the other side. Serve with butter and honey, stewed apple or, for a special occasion, smoked salmon and sour cream.

Rice Cakes

1 cup milk
1 cup cooked rice
pinch of salt

2 eggs, separated
1 tablespoon melted butter
1 cup flour

Combine milk, rice and salt in a bowl. Beat the egg yolks, add them to the rice and then mix in the butter and flour. Beat the egg whites until stiff and fold gently into the mixture. Drop spoonfuls into a hot greased pan and cook until the top is bubbling and the underside is golden. Turn over and brown other side. Serve warm with butter and cinnamon sugar.

'A good way to make use of leftover rice.'

Cinnamon Breakfast Cakes

1¹/₂ tablespoons butter
2 cups plain flour
1¹/₂ tablespoons sugar
1 tablespoon baking powder

1 egg
1 cup milk
2 teaspoons ground cinnamon

Rub the butter into the flour, stir in the sugar and baking powder, and mix into a dough with the egg and milk. Form into flat cakes, brush over with a little extra milk and sprinkle with the cinnamon. Dot with butter and bake in a hot oven for about 20 minutes. Cut open, spread with butter, and serve at once.

'If any are left, they are good split and toasted.'

CHILDREN'S MEALS
About the best arrangements for children attending school is to give them a generous and wholesome breakfast at eight o'clock of oatmeal porridge, scones, or bread and butter or jam, with a cup of coffee or milk . . . Honey is excellent for the little ones, and golden syrup is a pleasant change. For the morning meal boiled rice, germia, or bread and milk can take the place of porridge when preferred. I would warn mothers that oatmeal does not always agree with children, indeed there are some constitutions it decidedly disagrees with. Stewed fruit, poached eggs, omelets, all are excellent for the morning meal, with cocoa, chocolate, coffee, or milk for beverages.
The Antipodean Cookery Book,
1895

COOKERY FOR COTTAGE
AND VILLA HOMES
As a nation, we have been
accused of being exceedingly
bad cooks, and there probably
was considerable truth in the
statement. Large fat chops fried
in a frying pan, tough mutton
roasted to a cinder, and salt
beef, stringy and hard, formed
the staple fare in too many
homes; but several changes
have taken place of late years,
one, in the rising price of meat,
making it incumbent that
housewives should practice
economy, and have more made-
up dishes; another, in that girls,
in the State schools at least, are
being taught to cook.
The Melbourne Cookery Book,
c. 1900

Pumpkin Muffins

1¹/₂ cups self-raising flour   *1 egg*

¹/₂ teaspoon salt   *¹/₄ cup vegetable oil*

¹/₄ teaspoon nutmeg   *¹/₂ cup cooked, mashed*

¹/₄ teaspoon mixed spice   *pumpkin*

¹/₂ cup soft brown sugar   *¹/₂ cup milk*

¹/₂ cup sultanas

Sift flour, salt and spices into a bowl, then stir in sugar
and sultanas. Beat the egg, add the oil, pumpkin and
milk, and blend well.

Add pumpkin mixture to the dry ingredients and mix
thoroughly. Turn into 12 well-greased patty tins and
bake in a hot oven for 20 minutes, or until puffed and
golden. Serve at once.

Zwieback or Dry Toast

Cut slices of stale bread (white or wholemeal) in half,
place on tins and bake in a moderate oven until evenly
browned and crisp throughout. Store in an airtight jar
or tin.

VARIATIONS

Cream Toast: moisten slices of zwieback in hot water,
sprinkle with a little salt, and drizzle a teaspoon or two
of 'sweet' cream over each slice.

Tomato Toast: stew 2 cups of tomatoes in a little butter
and then drain off any excess moisture. Bring to the boil
and thicken with 1 tablespoon cornflour mixed with a
little cold water until smooth. Season the mixture with
salt and a little cream or butter. Moisten slices of
zwieback in hot milk before pouring tomatoes over.

THE BREAKFAST TABLE

The Americans are first-rate hands at the display and fixings they put on the table; but we believe that the Scotch exceed all other nations, in the variety at this repast, and the goodness of the viands. Coffee is the liquid for this meal; eschew tea by all means, unless for an exercise or a journey, and then a glass of mild ale is not to be disregarded. For training to obtain a good wind in walking, running, boxing, riding, or rowing, there is no breakfast more wholesome than oatmeal porridge, so says RURAL FIELD SPORTS, and it is very good tact to commence the breakfast with a plateful on any other occasion . . .

The CARTE of a well-appointed breakfast is as follows: — On a table, where everything should be neat and simple, there should be as many different kinds of rolls as the person who prepares them is able to make. These should differ from each other as much in form as in taste, and on the side table there should be some cold dishes, such as fowls, pheasants, partridges, tongue, ham, cold pâtes, &c. Few persons are displeased at seeing a slight sprinkling of hot dishes, as mutton kidneys, new-laid eggs, eggs and bacon, boiled cutlets, larks À LA MINUTE, devilled fowl, &c.; in fact, all that is generally considered as constituting a DÉJEÛNER À LA FOURCHETTE, observing that the hot meats ought not to be served till the guests are at table. Tea (green and black separately), coffee, and chocolate, should also be served.

The English and Australian Cookery Book, 1864

BREAKFAST ETIQUETTE

Always come to the meal table in as tidy and neat a costume as possible. Dressing-gowns are not permissible for a gentleman at breakfast, nor should anyone come in his shirt-sleeves. It is not correct to read telegrams, letters, books, or the newspaper at a meal table if others are present. If a telegram or a letter must be read, ask permission to do so first.

Australian Etiquette, 1960

STEWED FRUIT

The flavour of stewed fruit is often much injured by over-cooking. Any stewing beyond what is requisite to induce softness is bad. A good way in which to stew fruit is to prepare a syrup at the rate of 1 lb of sugar to 1 pint of water. Set this syrup to boil in a copper or enamelled pan, and when boiling, immerse in it the fruit in hand, lifting it out with a wooden spoon whenever brought to the point of breaking; using the same syrup to cook a fresh supply, and pouring it over the fruit when all is done. Fruit thus cooked has a freshness and delicacy never realised when it is stewed to pulp. Rhubarb, for instance, will be found far more palatable when thus cooked so lightly as to preserve its form. Oranges, too, peeled and separated into sections are delicious when treated in the same way.

The Hobart Cookery Book, 1900

French Toast

3 eggs, lightly beaten
1/2 teaspoon salt
2 tablespoons sugar
1 cup milk
6 slices stale bread

Mix the eggs, salt, sugar and milk, and place in a shallow dish. Soak the bread in this mixture until soft, turning once. Cook on a hot, greased skillet, turning to brown each side. Serve with grilled tomatoes and bacon, or sprinkle with a mixture of cinnamon and sugar.

Welsh Rarebit

1 cup grated tasty cheese
6 tablespoons beer
2 tablespoons butter
2 teaspoons French mustard
salt and pepper
pinch of cayenne

Combine the cheese and beer in a heavy-based saucepan. Stir over a very low heat until cheese has melted and mixture is creamy. Add butter, mustard, salt, pepper and cayenne, and return to stove to reheat (but do not allow to boil). Serve on triangles of buttered toast or fried bread.

Scrambled Eggs

2 eggs per person
1 tablespoon water or cream
for each egg
salt and pepper

butter
finely chopped chives or
parsley for garnish

Beat eggs, water or cream and seasonings with a fork until well mixed. Heat a generous nut of butter in a pan, add egg mixture and stir over a very gentle heat until thick and creamy but a little undercooked. Stir in a little extra butter before serving, and garnish with chives or parsley.

VARIATIONS

Add 1 teaspoon curry powder for every 2 eggs, before cooking. Other flavourings (1 tablespoon per 2 eggs) include grated cheese, fresh herbs (especially chives or tarragon) or strips of ham or smoked salmon.
Scotch Woodcock: add a pinch of cayenne to the egg mixture before cooking and serve on toast fingers spread with anchovy paste. Garnish with finely chopped parsley.

Dainty Eggs

3 tablespoons chopped parsley
3 tablespoons finely minced
ham

6 eggs

Grease 6 ramekins and sprinkle with chopped parsley. Place some ham in the bottom of each dish, break an egg into it, and then bake in a hot oven for 10 minutes or until the egg is set. Turn out on rounds of buttered toast, and serve very hot.

VARIATION

Sprinkle ramekins with fresh breadcrumbs instead of parsley, omit the ham and sprinkle grated cheese and a pinch of cayenne over the eggs.

EGGS AND PUMPKIN TOPS

Pluck a large quantity of the shoots of a pumpkin vine; wash well and boil in salted water, to which a pinch of soda has been added; when soft strain thoroughly and press in a colander, then return it to the saucepan and add a little piece of butter and seasoning of pepper; have ready some buttered toast cut in squares and place in a vegetable dish. Just before the pumpkin tops are ready to strain, poach some eggs nicely; and when the greens are placed neatly on the buttered toast, arrange the poached eggs on top and serve.

CHOCOLATE

Chocolate is a rich breakfast beverage. Do not grate it, but cut the quantity required, and boil it in water. To an ounce of chocolate put an ounce and a half of boiling water; add cream or milk. Do not allow it to boil over if you desire the flavour to be preserved, and it must not be boiled a second time. The prepared homoeopathic cocoa is highly spoken of as an excellent preparation for an early meal, wholesome, devoid of fatty matter, and digestible. Messrs Fry and Son's homoeopathic cocoa is recommended for invalids and persons subject to dyspepsia. Messrs Fry, of London and Bristol, were awarded medals at the Exhibitions of London, Paris, and New York, so that their preparation has a world-wide celebrity.

The English and Australian Cookery Book, 1864

POACHED EGGS

This is a very difficult operation in cookery. It has been said that one of the London clubs in want of a cook, put the first preliminary question – 'Can you boil a potato?' But a more proper query would be – can you poach eggs properly? To proceed – put in a stewpan a pint of water, with half a table-spoonful of salt, and three of vinegar; when simmering break in the eggs, and let them remain until the yolk is set. Serve on toast or spinach. If the cook cannot do this well, he had better have recourse to a tin stand, which contains a receptacle for each egg, and the stand is immersed in the pan containing boiling water until the egg is sufficiently done.

The English and Australian Cookery Book, 1864

TEMPTING
BREAKFAST DISH
Take 3 or 4 fresh herrings, cleaned thoroughly; split them open, carefully remove the backbone, and wipe dry. Prepare a forcemeat by soaking a few breadcrumbs in a little milk. Beat them up well, and add about 2 tablespoons of shrimps, chopped finely; season to taste with cayenne and salt, and flavour with a few drops of anchovy essence; mix well. Spread the forcemeat over the herrings, and roll them up securely. Fasten with tiny skewers. Brush them over with beaten eggs, and roll them in raspings; place in a buttered baking tin, put a few dabs of butter here and there, and bake in a moderate oven for about 30 minutes. Serve hot.

Potato Triangles

¾ cup flour
½ teaspoon salt
1 teaspoon baking powder
½ cup butter

2 cups mashed potato
3 egg yolks
½ cup milk

Sift the flour, salt and baking powder into a bowl, then rub butter in lightly. Add potato and mix until smooth. Beat egg yolks, add to the milk and stir into potato mixture to form a stiff paste. Roll out about 1 cm thick, cut into triangles and bake in a hot oven for about 20 minutes. Split open, butter well and serve hot.

Kedgeree

½ onion, chopped
1 teaspoon curry powder
  (optional)
2 tablespoons (or more) butter
2 cups cooked long-grain rice
1 cup cooked, flaked smoked
  haddock (or 250 g canned
  salmon)

2 hard-boiled eggs, chopped
1 tablespoon chopped parsley
salt and pepper

Sauté the onion (and curry powder if used) in 2 teaspoons of the butter until transparent. Stir in the rice and the rest of the butter, and mix well over a very gentle heat. Add the fish and eggs, stirring gently with a fork to distribute them evenly through the rice. Add the parsley, salt and pepper and reheat gently. Stir in more butter before serving if desired, as kedgeree should be very buttery.

Fish Hash

*1 cup cooked fish, skin and
  bones removed*
2 cups mashed potato
1 egg

1 tablespoon melted butter
2 tablespoons cream
pepper to taste

Combine the fish and potato, heat a little, then add the egg, butter and cream. Beat until very light, and then fry lightly in butter. Fold like an omelette, and serve on a heated dish.

Zucchini Pikelets

1 cup grated zucchini
*1 tablespoon orange or lemon
  juice*
1 cup self-raising flour

1 tablespoon sugar
1 egg
³/₄ cup milk
2 teaspoons butter

Steam grated zucchini in the orange or lemon juice until wilted. Combine flour, sugar, egg and milk, then stir in the zucchini. Grease pan, bring to medium heat and drop in spoonfuls of the batter. Turn pikelets when bubbles appear and brown on the other side.

COFFEE BENEFICIAL

Coffee is said to be an antidote to the gout and rheumatism. A case is mentioned in the *Pharmaceutical Journal*, of a gentleman having had the gout for twenty years who was completely cured by the use of coffee. In asthma it has been found particularly serviceable, and it is extolled in gangrene of the extremities in drunkards. Calculous complaints are scarcely known in France and Turkey, where coffee is the principal beverage of the people.
The English and Australian Cookery Book, 1864

Luncheon Dishes

SOME OF THE MORE perceptive newcomers to Australia last century were so appalled by the heavy luncheon dishes placed before them that they felt compelled to protest. One was Dr Philip Muskett, a vigorous campaigner for improved diet:

> There is one very important matter which unquestionably requires to have special attention drawn to it. I refer to the customary Australian mid-day meal. Strange to say, all through the hot season, as well as the rest of the year, this consists in most cases of a heavy repast always comprising meat. Why, even in the cooler months, a ponderous meal of this kind is not required! My own views are that meat in the middle of the day is quite unnecessary, and, indeed, during the hot months actually prejudicial. Most people in Australia, after a fair trial, will find that a lunch of some warm soup, with a course perhaps of some fish, and vegetables, or salad, or whatever it may be to follow, will not only be ample, but will give them a sensation of buoyancy in the afternoon they never before experienced.

It has taken us a hundred years to decide that we generally prefer lighter lunches and that we enjoy them more if we are lunching outdoors. When the weather is cooler, many of the recipes originally meant as entrées – made from eggs, from cheese or from unexpected combinations of vegetables – can be enjoyed for lunch, perhaps with a salad. But how, after such dishes, did earlier generations have room for the hot main course that usually followed?

ON LUNCHEONS
A person who partakes of a luncheon cannot possibly enjoy his dinner; and any one eating supper must loathe his breakfast, which ought to be the principal meal of the day. The utmost limit that we can advise in either case is a glass of sherry and a biscuit. 'Nimrod' writes, that a hot luncheon is a most destructive meal; and half the young men who lose their health or their lives in the East Indies, are destroyed by the excitement of hot luncheons, followed by still hotter dinners. Hook describes a stand-up supper, in 'Gilbert Gurney', as 'tables against the wall, covered with cold negus and warm ice, where men, women and children take perpendicular refreshment, like so many horses with their noses in the manger'.
The English and Australian Cookery Book, 1864

Picnic Eggs

6 hard-boiled eggs
1/4 cup cream
1 teaspoon butter
1 teaspoon chopped parsley
1 teaspoon finely chopped onion

1 tablespoon mashed sardines (or use finely chopped ham or anchovies)
pinch of salt

Cut the eggs in half, take out the yolks and mash them with the cream or milk. Add other ingredients, mix well and fill the whites with the mixture. Garnish with sprigs of parsley and serve with slices of thin brown bread and butter. If using the ham or anchovies, add a little prepared mustard to the filling mixture.

Eggs à la Suisse

6 slices Gruyère cheese
6 eggs
pepper and salt

1/4 teaspoon ground nutmeg
1/2 cup cream
4–6 tablespoons grated cheese

Cover the bottom of a greased pie dish with the slices of cheese. Break in the eggs without disturbing the yolks, season with pepper, salt and nutmeg and pour cream over. Sprinkle with grated cheese, then bake in a moderate–hot oven for about 10 minutes. Serve with thin, hot buttered toast.

Scalloped Eggs

6 hard-boiled eggs · salt and pepper
1–2 cups fine breadcrumbs · 1 cup milk

Shell the eggs and cut into thin slices. Put a layer of breadcrumbs in a greased, deep dish, followed by a layer of the sliced eggs. Sprinkle with salt and pepper, then repeat the layers of breadcrumbs and eggs until the dish is filled, finishing with a layer of crumbs. Heat the milk, pour into the dish, sprinkle a few more crumbs over and bake in a moderate oven until top is lightly browned.

An Omelette

4 eggs · 1 tablespoon butter
salt and pepper
1 tablespoon milk or cream

Break the eggs into a bowl and season with salt and pepper. Add the water, milk or cream, and beat lightly with a fork or whisk until just blended. Bring the omelette pan to a medium heat, add the butter and shake pan so that bottom is evenly coated. As soon as butter starts to sizzle, add the egg mixture and stir for a few seconds. As the omelette begins to set, lift the edges with a spatula to allow any liquid egg to run under. The omelette is ready when all the excess liquid has been absorbed but the eggs are still moist.

VARIATIONS

Asparagus Omelette: boil or steam 6–8 young asparagus stems until just tender. Cut into bite-sized pieces and add to the egg mixture before cooking.

Herb Omelette: add 1 tablespoon chopped fresh herbs (especially tarragon, lemon thyme or chives) to the egg mixture.

EGGS A LA NESSELRODE

Take and prepare a savoury chestnut purée, put it into a forcing bag to which you have attached a plain or fancy tube, and make a fairly bold border on a buttered gratin dish. Put about 2 tablespoonsful of cream in the dish, upon this break carefully 4 or 5 fresh eggs. Season with salt and pepper and bake in the oven till the eggs are set. Serve hot.

SWISS OMELETTE

To 2 oz of grated Parmesan cheese add 2 oz of melted butter, 1/2 oz of finely chopped parsley, 1 oz of breadcrumbs, 1/4 pint of fresh milk, and 4 beaten eggs. Fry in the usual way with a little butter in the pan, which must be properly heated before putting mixture in. To the mixture add, before cooking, a little pepper and salt.

ABOUT SOUFFLÉS
Soufflés and omelettes may be classed in much the same category, having many similar characteristics. Neither will bear keeping when made, both are made of eggs, and both are more of a *bonne bouche*, or tit-bit, than anything else. At least, one would hardly put either in front of a very hungry man.
The Antipodean Cookery Book, 1895

Cheese Soufflé

4 tablespoons butter	6 egg whites
3 tablespoons flour	1 cup grated parmesan
1¼ cups milk	salt and pepper
5 egg yolks	pinch of ground nutmeg

Melt the butter in a saucepan. Add the flour, blend well together and gradually add the milk. Bring to the boil and simmer until sauce thickens. Remove from heat, add egg yolks one at a time and then the cheese. Blend well and return to heat until cheese melts. Beat egg whites to a stiff froth, fold into cheese mixture, pile into a greased deep dish and bake in a moderate oven for 25–30 minutes or until puffed and golden. Serve at once.

A blue cheese such as Stilton, Danish Blue or Castello may be substituted for the parmesan.

Filled Pancakes

1¼ cups flour	1 tablespoon oil
½ teaspoon salt	½ cup water
1¼ cups milk	1 egg

Sift the flour and salt into a bowl and gradually add the milk and water, beating constantly. Add the eggs and oil, beat again until smooth and then set aside for at least 1 hour. When ready to cook, lightly grease a pan and place over a medium heat. Pour about 2 tablespoons of batter into the pan and tilt gently until surface of pan is covered thinly. When bottom is brown, turn pancake with a spatula and cook briefly on the other side. Pile onto a plate and repeat the process until all the batter has been used. To fill, return pancake to pan, add 2–3 tablespoons of filling, reheat (this will take about 2 minutes), then roll up and serve.

FILLINGS

Ham and cheese: mix ¹/₂ cup each of grated cheese and chopped ham.

Seafood: combine 1 cup cooked, flaked white fish (or use mussels, crab or prawns) with ¹/₂ cup sour cream, 2 tablespoons chopped parsley and ¹/₄ cup grated cheese.

Chicken: mix 1 cup cooked chopped chicken into ¹/₂ cup White Sauce (page 104) and stir in salt, pepper and nutmeg plus 2 egg yolks.

Spinach: mix 1 cup chopped spinach (fresh or frozen), ¹/₂ cup ricotta and 2 tablespoons grated parmesan into the egg mixture before cooking.

Little Farmhouse Pasties

1 carrot	*2 tablespoons chopped parsley*
1 parsnip	*¹/₄ teaspoon mixed dried herbs*
1 potato	*salt and pepper*
1 onion	*250 g shortcrust pastry*
500 g minced lamb or beef	*milk or beaten egg to glaze*

Grate the carrot, parsnip and potato, and chop the onion. Combine the vegetables with the meat, parsley, herbs, salt and pepper. Roll out the pastry and cut into circles about the size of a small saucer. Put a spoonful of filling onto each circle, moisten the edges and fold over to form a crescent. Crimp edges together, brush top with milk or beaten egg, and bake in a moderate–hot oven for about 45 minutes or until golden-brown.

VARIATION

Devonshire Squabs: proceed as above, but substitute a filling of equal parts (about 250 g each) of minced pork and chopped apple, plus a little finely chopped onion, pepper and salt, and a pinch of dried sage.

Veal and Ham Pie

500 g cooked veal
½ cup chopped ham or bacon
3 hard-boiled eggs, sliced
1 teaspoon grated lemon rind
1 onion, chopped
1 tablespoon chopped parsley

salt and pepper
pinch of ground nutmeg
about 1 cup chicken stock
250 g flaky pastry
beaten egg to glaze

Chop or shred the veal and layer into a greased pie dish with the ham or bacon and the sliced egg, sprinkling in the onion, lemon rind and seasonings as you go. Pour in stock, to come two-thirds up the side of the dish, cover with flaky pastry, glaze with beaten egg and bake in a hot oven for 30 minutes or until pastry is browned. Lower heat and bake for a further 15–20 minutes.

Chicken or rabbit pieces may be substituted for the veal.

Egg and Bacon Pie

250 g shortcrust pastry
4 bacon rashers
6 eggs

salt and pepper
2 tablespoons chopped parsley
milk or beaten egg to glaze

Cut pastry into two and roll out. Line pie plate with half the pastry, lay bacon rashers over and then break in the eggs, spaced evenly around the plate. Prick the egg yolks so that they will spread during cooking. Sprinkle with chopped parsley, and salt and pepper to taste. Top with the remaining pastry, trim with a sharp knife and press edges well together. Brush with milk or beaten egg, bake in a moderate oven for 45 minutes, and serve cold.

A SIMPLE CREAM CHEESE
Put a little salt into 1 pint of sweet thick cream, stir into it, having previously slightly warmed it, a tablespoon of rennet, and pour the whole into a scalded linen cloth, which has been laid on a soup plate. Let it remain in a warm kitchen for 12 hours, then change it into a clean cloth, wetted as before, and tie it up and hang it in a cool larder, change the cloth daily for three days, when the cheese should be firm. Smack it into shape and lay on a clean plate, turn it daily until it looks buttery, then serve it on dried green leaves or in a rush basket.

THE LUNCHEON

Luncheon is a much more go-as-you-please function than a dinner. The INVITATION may be made either verbally, or by a little informal note, and the notice may be given either a couple of weeks ahead or the same number of days. Sometimes a lady may have a fixed day on which she is pleased to see visitors to lunch, say any Tuesday or Thursday. It is, of course, more courteous to drop a line to say you will be coming on that day, as she will then know how many to cater for. Hostesses are generally pleased if their gentlemen friends come in without notice, as the male element is generally lacking at these affairs. The TIME, unless it is expressly stated, to appear at these functions is half-past one. On arriving at the house, the gentleman is expected to leave his hat and stick in the hall, and the lady leaves her wraps, but keeps on her hat; her gloves are removed, or rolled-up, when she reaches the luncheon table. The GUESTS are shown into the drawing-room, where the HOSTESS is waiting to receive them. She shakes hands, and will probably introduce a few here and there. If the HOST is present, he leads the way with the most important lady; if he is absent, the HOSTESS leads the way. The ladies then follow without ceremony, and the gentlemen come in last of all. If any particular seat is indicated, of course it must be taken, but as a rule the GUESTS sit where they please. If anyone is late, he or she is shown straight into the dining room, and the hostess rises to greet a lady, but not a gentleman. A SERVANT usually waits at table, as at a dinner, but she may withdraw after each course has been served until rung for. Sometimes the host will serve the meat course, while his wife serves the vegetables, and the maid is rung for to change the plates at the end of each course. The same rules for serving the dishes are observed as at a dinner. When lunch is over, the signal to rise is given by the HOSTESS to the principal lady guest, and they return to the drawing-room, the gentlemen following if the host is absent; if he is present, they may linger for a little while to smoke. The GUESTS are not supposed to stay very long after the luncheon, unless they are specially invited to afternoon tea.

Australian Etiquette, 1960

Croquettes of Spinach and Cheese

1 bunch spinach, well washed
1½ cups ricotta or curd
  cheese
3 tablespoons flour
2–3 eggs

salt and pepper
1½ tablespoons grated
  parmesan
pinch of nutmeg
butter for serving

Steam the spinach, then drain thoroughly, pressing out all the excess moisture. Put in a blender with the remaining ingredients except the butter, then refrigerate until needed (for up to 12 hours). Form into small cylinders about 2 cm long and cook in plenty of boiling water: they will rise to the surface when done. Remove with a slotted spoon and serve with a little melted butter and a few torn leaves of basil.

Creamed Macaroni and Cheese

2 tablespoons butter
2 tablespoons flour
2½ cups milk
1½ cups macaroni

1 cup grated parmesan or
  tasty cheese
extra parmesan for baking

Boil macaroni in slightly salted water until just tender, then drain. Melt the butter in a pan, stir in the flour and then gradually add the milk. Simmer until sauce thickens, then stir in the macaroni. Finally add the parmesan, stir well and then pour into a greased gratin dish. Sprinkle with extra parmesan and bake in a moderate oven for about 30 minutes or until sides are bubbling and top is golden-brown.

HOT DRESSED CRAB
Pick all the flesh out of one medium crab and mix it in a basin with about a tablespoonful of butter, a saltspoonful of mustard, a little cayenne and salt; put into scallop shells, then moisten it all with vinegar. Cover with breadcrumbs and bake.

Marrow Croûtes

6 thick slices French bread
¹/₂ cup beef or veal marrow
yolks of 2 hard-boiled eggs
pinch of cayenne
salt and pepper to taste

1 tablespoon finely chopped
  parsley
¹/₂ teaspoon ground bay leaf
toasted breadcrumbs

Scoop out the centre of each bread round, leaving a thickish base and sides. Fry this croute in butter until golden on both sides. Mash the marrow with the egg yolks, then add the cayenne, salt and pepper, parsley and bayleaf. Mix well together and fill the centres of the croutons while they are hot. Sprinkle breadcrumbs over, dab a little butter on top and bake in a moderate oven for 10 minutes. Serve on a bed of watercress, and sprinkle some chopped parsley over.

A Cheese 'Casserole'

9 slices white bread (herb
  bread is delicious)
3 tablespoons finely chopped
  onion or spring onion
500 g grated tasty cheese
salt and pepper

4 eggs
3 cups milk
1 teaspoon Worcestershire
  sauce
1 teaspoon dry mustard

Trim the crusts off the bread and cut each slice into 3 strips. Arrange one-third of the bread at the bottom of a deep round casserole dish and sprinkle with one-third of the onion and then one-third of the cheese. Season, and repeat the layers. Beat the eggs with the milk, Worcestershire sauce and mustard. Pour over the casserole mixture and set aside for 8 hours (or overnight in the fridge). Bake uncovered in a moderate oven for 50 minutes until puffed and golden.

Artichokes with Oysters

6 artichoke hearts
1 cup White Sauce
 (page 104)
12 oysters
juice of 1 lemon

6 slices bread, fried in butter
1 tablespoon finely chopped
 parsley mashed into
2 tablespoons butter

Heat the artichoke hearts in the white sauce. Squeeze lemon juice over the oysters and stir them into the artichoke mixture. When the artichokes are quite hot, remove with a slotted spoon and place on the fried rounds of bread. Put 2 oysters on each, and top with the parsley butter. Pour the sauce round and serve at once.

 'A change may be made by serving minced chicken or game on the artichoke bottoms.'

Sweetbreads English-style

750 g sweetbreads
2 cups light chicken stock
juice of 1/2 lemon
250 g smoked bacon, thinly
 sliced and rind removed

1/2 cup breadcrumbs
1/4 cup butter
2 tablespoons finely chopped
 parsley
Bread Sauce (page 107)

Soak the sweetbreads in cold salted water for an hour. Drain and rinse them, then put into a saucepan and cover with the chicken stock. Simmer gently until beginning to whiten (about 5 minutes), then drain and press between two boards or plates for 1–2 hours (or overnight if more convenient). Cut the sweetbreads into thick slices, cut the bacon into longish pieces and wrap each around a sweetbread slice. Thread onto skewers and grill under a medium heat for 10–15 minutes. Brown the breadcrumbs in the butter, then roll the cooked skewers in them to coat. Scatter any remaining crumbs over, garnish with the parsley and serve immediately, with the bread sauce separately.

Croquettes of Brains

6 sets lamb brains
1 cup milk
pinch of salt
¹/₂ cup breadcrumbs, soaked
* in a little milk and squeezed*
1 tablespoon finely chopped
* parsley*

1 teaspoon each lemon juice
* and grated rind*
¹/₄ teaspoon ground nutmeg
salt and pepper
3 egg yolks
beaten egg and breadcrumbs
* for coating*

Soak the brains in cold water mixed with 2 teaspoons of vinegar for 1 hour. Place in a pan with the milk and salt, and simmer until no longer pink (about 15 minutes). Drain, mash or chop very finely and mix with the breadcrumbs, parsley, lemon juice and rind, nutmeg, salt and pepper. Bind with the egg yolks, then set aside for 30 minutes. Form into balls, dip into the beaten egg and then the breadcrumbs, and fry (or bake in a buttered dish in a hot oven) until golden-brown.

'Solomongundy'

1 cooked chicken, skin
* removed*
1 lettuce, shredded
1 cup blanched French beans
¹/₂ cup sliced gherkins or dill
* pickles*
8 anchovy fillets
¹/₂ cup grapes

4 hard-boiled eggs, quartered
¹/₂ cup flaked almonds
¹/₃ cup stoned raisins
1 large cup oil-and-vinegar
* dressing*
1 tablespoon chopped mixed
* herbs*
juice and rind of 1 lemon

Slice the chicken breast and leg meat thinly. Place the lettuce on a large platter and arrange the salad items over it in rows or clusters. Check the dressing for seasoning, then stir in the herbs and lemon juice and rind. Pour over the salad and toss everything together just before serving.

Cauliflower with Shrimp Sauce

1 medium cauliflower, left
   whole or broken into florets,
   as preferred
1 tablespoon butter
1 tablespoon flour
1½ cups fish stock (optional:
   see below)
½ cup cream

1 cup shelled shrimps
2 tablespoons dry sherry or
   white wine
1 tablespoon grated parmesan
1 teaspoon prepared mustard
salt and pepper
pinch of grated nutmeg

Boil or steam cauliflower until just tender. Drain,
reserving 2 cups of the cooking liquid, and place in a
greased dish. Melt the butter in a saucepan and stir in
the flour. Gradually add the cauliflower water (or fish
stock) and the cream and cook gently, stirring, until
smooth and slightly thickened. Stir in the shrimps,
sherry or wine, cheese and mustard, season with salt,
pepper and nutmeg, and pour over the cauliflower.
Bake in a moderate oven for 10–15 minutes or until
heated through.

   Whole miniature cauliflowers (1 per person) may be
used instead: serve in individual ramekins, with triangles
of fried bread tucked around the side.

Soups

AUSTRALIA'S EARLY SETTLERS all brought with them their favourite soup recipes, which were handed on from one generation to the next. While many of the ingredients for the pioneers' national dishes were unobtainable in the Antipodes, the basic elements of traditional 'local' soups were – and still are – universal. The Scots could continue to make Scotch Broth: dried peas and barley were soaked overnight, boiling water was added the next day, and chopped neck mutton, diced carrots, turnips and onions were thrown in, the whole lot being simmered at the back of the stove or over the campfire until needed, when some finely shredded cabbage heart was added. It was a meal in itself! Welsh settlers, too, continued to make their great standby, a rich white soup with milk, potatoes and lots of chopped leeks. And the Italians could still concoct Minestrone, brimming with the varied produce from their superb vegetable gardens, and a handful of home-made pasta tossed in.

With the coming of soup cubes, cans and packets, there was a move away from the tedious chopping up and long simmering of vegetables and other ingredients. Now soup could be made in a minute, in even less time than it took to open a tin. More recently, however, tastes have again changed: 'instant soup' cubes were found by many cooks to be too salty and too strongly flavoured, and the stockpot has come back into its own, particularly during winter weekends.

Of course there have always been soups that could be made very quickly. Mrs Maclurcan, for one, gave a recipe for Oyster Soup 'made in a quarter of an hour', but as it called for six dozen oysters this puts it beyond the resources of most households today. Equally impractical is the recipe that begins 'Take one dozen parrots, well plucked and cleaned . . .'.

CLEAR SOUP

Strain your stock and then add to the liquor the whites and shells of 2 eggs, well beaten together. Allow to simmer, but not boil, for half an hour, strain through a fine towel or a felt bag, then add a gill of sherry and a teaspoonful of tarragon vinegar.

First Beef Stock

2 kg shin of beef	1/2 head celery, chopped
3 litres water	bouquet garni
1 tablespoon salt	4 allspice berries
2 onions, chopped	12 peppercorns
2 carrots, chopped	6 cloves

Chop the beef and bones into smallish pieces and place in a large pot with the water. Bring slowly to the boil, add the salt and skim well. Add the remaining ingredients and simmer, covered, for 2–3 hours. Allow to cool, strain, and refrigerate overnight. Remove any fat before using.

'Palestine' Soup

4 tablespoons butter	salt and pepper
2 rashers lean bacon (or	cayenne
1/2 cup chopped ham)	6 cups light chicken stock
1 onion, chopped	2 tablespoons chopped parsley
1 clove garlic, chopped	1/4 cup cream
1 stick celery, chopped	
500 g Jerusalem artichokes, peeled	

Put butter, bacon, onion, garlic and celery in a pan and cook gently, without browning, for 5 minutes. Add the artichokes, salt, pepper, cayenne and stock, and simmer until tender. Sieve, or purée in a blender, then return to the pan to reheat. Stir in the parsley and cream just before serving with snippets of fried bread.

Scotch Broth

1 kg lamb breast or neck,
  trimmed of excess fat
2 tablespoons pearl barley
8 cups water
1 tablespoon butter
1 rasher bacon, chopped
1/2 cup diced carrot

1/2 cup diced turnip
1/2 cup finely chopped onion
1/2 cup peas
1/4 cup finely sliced cabbage
1 tablespoon chopped parsley
pepper and salt

Put lamb and barley in a large pot, cover with the water,
bring to boil and simmer for 1 1/2 hours or until meat is
very tender. Remove meat from stock and discard
bones. Allow to cool and spoon off any fat. Fry the
bacon in butter until fat runs, then add the carrot,
turnip, onion, peas and cabbage. Add stock and meat,
reheat and stir in parsley, pepper and salt just before
serving.

Lettuce Soup

3 tablespoons butter
1 small lettuce, shredded
2 spring onions, chopped
grated rind of 1/2 lemon
1 sprig herbs, including
  chervil if possible

3 1/4 cups light chicken stock
lemon juice to taste
2 egg yolks
1/2 cup cream

Melt the butter in a pan and add the lettuce, spring
onions, lemon peel and herbs. Cook gently for about
5 minutes, add the stock, and simmer for another 10–20
minutes. Purée in a blender, then return to pan to
reheat. Add lemon juice to taste, the beaten egg yolks
and the cream, and whisk until thickened (do not let the
soup boil again, as it will curdle).

PETERBOROUGH SOUP
Mr Baron Bramwell lately tried
the case of Wilkins *v.* Smith in
the Court of Exchequer, which
was an action for libel, brought
by the proprietor of the
refreshment rooms at the
Peterborough railway station.
On the publication of the report
of the journey the following
day, the reporter said he trusted
His Royal Highness had not
tasted the 'detestable juice of
horse-beans, which is retailed to
Her Majesty's lieges at that
station at a shilling a plate'. The
defendant declined to
apologise, and the jury gave a
verdict of 25 pounds damages.
*The English and Australian
Cookery Book*, 1864

ABOUT SOUPS AND PURÉES

The first subject upon which I wish to speak to the student in cookery is soups and purées. I do not think that in ordinary English and Colonial households importance enough is attached to soup as a food. During cold weather a plateful of warm soup stimulates digestion, and is quite an appetizer for dinner; and in summertime one would scarcely believe how refreshing a plateful of soup, just warm, is. Now, in an ordinary way, expensive soups are not necessary, and when two or three joints are cooked in the course of the week, soup sufficient for three or four persons every day may be easily made without buying soup meat . . .

Both soups and purées should be served very hot. Nothing is more disagreeable than luke-warm soup. The reason why soup is not so popular with us as it is in France and other countries is because it is so often served nearly cold and greasy. I cannot conclude these remarks better than by quoting a sentence from a health lecture recently delivered by C. R. Blackett, Esq. He says:— 'How seldom do we find the delicious soups and potages of the French upon an English table, and yet really no dinner ought to be considered complete without a soup. Any intelligent housewife would soon discover endless ways of varying them with different herbs and vegetables. Sauces spoil soup. Let them be avoided. A good soup or potage at the beginning of a dinner is Nature's teaching; and, if generally adopted, would do more, I believe, to check and prevent the craving for stimulants than anything else. It is in itself a powerful stimulant; it affords just that gentle excitement to the stomach which prepares it for the more solid food to follow.

The Kingswood Cookery Book, n.d.

Carrot Soup with Orange

2 tablespoons butter
1 small onion, chopped
1 stick celery, chopped
1 sprig herbs (e.g. chervil, thyme)
750 g carrots, chopped
6 cups chicken stock
salt and pepper
a little ground nutmeg
$^1/_2$ cup orange juice
1 tablespoon grated orange rind
cream for serving

Melt the butter in a large pan, add the onion and celery, and cook gently for 5 minutes. Add the herbs and carrots, cover the pan and continue to cook very gently for a further 10 minutes, shaking the pan occasionally to prevent the contents sticking. Add the stock and seasoning, and simmer until tender (about 20 minutes). Purée in a blender, return to the pan and stir in the orange juice and rind. Reheat, and serve with a dollop of cream in each bowl.

Mushroom Soup with Mustard

2 tablespoons butter
1 small onion, chopped
250 g mushrooms, chopped
3 cups chicken stock
$^1/_2$ cup double cream
2 tablespoons dry sherry or Madeira
1 dessertspoon French mustard
salt and pepper

Melt the butter in a pan until it begins to colour. Add the onions and mushrooms and toss them in the butter until they are only just tender. Add the stock and sherry or Madeira, bring to the boil and add the mustard. Remove from heat, allow to cool a little and then purée in a blender. Add the cream, adjust the seasoning, reheat and serve.

BOUILLON AUX HERBES
(Strengthening)
Take leaves of sorrel, leeks, lettuce, purslain, and chervil, about two handfuls of each; pick and wash them; add salt, some fresh butter; boil together in three pints of water till it is reduced to half; take it off and strain it. If you like you can add the yolks of two eggs, beaten with a spoonful of cream.
The English and Australian Cookery Book, 1864

Fresh Pea Soup

4 tablespoons butter
250 g shelled peas
1 small lettuce, shredded
1 onion, chopped
1 sprig mint

4 cups chicken or light bacon
stock
pinch of salt
1 teaspoon sugar

Melt the butter, add the peas, lettuce, onion and mint, and steam gently together until the vegetables are soft. Remove the mint and set aside 2–3 tablespoons of the peas. Purée the remaining vegetables in a blender with enough stock to make a thick cream. Return to the saucepan, add the salt and sugar, reheat and add the reserved peas. Serve with snippets of fried bread, and crisp-cooked bacon pieces if liked.

Cold Fruit Soup

1 kg ripe fruit (e.g. cherries, apples, plums, pears or berries)
2 cups water
2 tablespoons lemon juice
1 stick cinnamon
sugar to taste

1 tablespoon cornflour, dissolved in a little water
2 tablespoons white wine
sour cream to serve
1 tablespoon grated lemon rind

Put the fruit in an enamel or aluminium saucepan with the water, lemon juice and cinnamon stick, and simmer until fruit is tender. Strain through a sieve to catch the stones or seeds, then purée in a blender with the cooking liquid. Sweeten to taste. Put purée in a saucepan, add dissolved cornflour and bring to boil. Simmer until soup begins to thicken, then add the wine. Remove from heat and refrigerate. Serve topped with sour cream and a sprinkle of lemon rind.

BISQUE

A Bisque is a purée of any shell fish. Take a large Australian crayfish, cooked, put on one side the claws and tail, pound the rest smooth with 2 tablespoonfuls of butter, put in a casserole with half-pint of water, bring to the boil, then pass through a wire sieve, put it back in the casserole with 2 large slices of toasted bread (only lightly toasted). When the bread is soft, pass all through a sieve again. Put back into the casserole, and add enough fish stock to make it the consistency of a purée. Before taking off the fire add the chopped up meat of the tail and claws, and let simmer 5 minutes, then serve with fried bread; just before serving half-cup of cream may be added.

The Kookaburra Cookery Book, 1911

An Elegant Beetroot Soup

1 kg large beetroot, cooked,
  skinned and coarsely grated
1/2 cup grated carrot
2 tablespoons butter
6 cups beef or chicken stock

salt and pepper
chopped parsley and chives
  for garnish
sour cream for serving

Heat butter in a pan, add grated beetroot and carrot, and sugar to taste, then simmer gently for a few minutes. Remove from heat. Heat stock in a large pan and add the vegetable mixture, salt and pepper. Serve immediately with a scattering of parsley and chives and a swirl of sour cream in each bowl.

Welsh Leek and Potato Soup

4 leeks, trimmed and sliced
500 g potatoes, peeled and
  chopped
1 onion, chopped
1 1/2 tablespoons butter
6 cups chicken stock
1 cup cream

1/4 teaspoon ground nutmeg
salt and pepper
3 tablespoons finely chopped
  parsley
a few chives, snipped into
  5-cm lengths

Melt the butter in a large saucepan, add the leeks, potatoes and onions, and cook over a low heat until the onion is transparent. Add stock and simmer gently for about 30 minutes or until potato is tender. Blend or purée the vegetables with some or all of the stock (depending on the consistency preferred), then stir in the cream and seasonings. Return to pan, reheat and serve in individual bowls. 'Croutons and crisp bacon pieces may be handed separately.'

Hare Soup

1 hare or rabbit, jointed	small bouquet of herbs (thyme,
8 cups bacon stock (or water	parsley, bay leaf, oregano)
with a few bacon bones)	2 teaspoons salt
125 g lean ham	1 tablespoon butter
2 onions	1 tablespoon flour
2 teaspoons peppercorns	1 wineglass port
2 teaspoons cloves	1 teaspoon redcurrant jelly

Put the hare or rabbit into a saucepan with the stock, ham, onions, peppercorns, cloves, herbs and salt. Simmer gently for 4 hours, then strain and allow to cool. Melt the butter with the flour in a saucepan, and when smooth gradually add the strained cooking liquor, wine and redcurrant jelly. Stir constantly while bringing almost to the boil. Small Forcemeat Balls (see page 115) may be added a few minutes before the soup is served.

Mulligatawny Soup

2 onions, sliced	2 tablespoons curry powder
2 cloves garlic, chopped	(or to taste)
3 rashers bacon	$3/4$ cup yoghurt
2 tablespoons butter	6 cups water
1 small chicken, cut into	pinch of salt
serving pieces	juice of 1 lemon

Brown the onions, garlic and bacon in the butter, then add the chicken pieces. Cook gently for a few minutes, then add the curry powder and yoghurt and cook for a few minutes more. Add water and simmer until chicken is tender. Skim carefully and add salt and lemon juice. Serve with boiled rice.

'In warm climates, hot curries and mulligatawny soups are always dishes in request; the former a favourite with the matutinal meal.'

BECHE-DE-MER SOUP
Put $1/2$ lb Beche-de-Mer into warm water and allow to soak for 24 hours. Scrape thoroughly and wash well. Put in a saucepan to simmer till quite tender. Have ready a good stock in which 2 carrots and a piece of green ginger has been cooked. Chop Beche-de-Mer very fine and add to strained stock. When ready to serve add $1/4$ cup of sherry.
The Schauer Australian Cookery Book, 1946

Savouries and Beverages

SAVOURIES OFTEN MERITED a chapter of their own in early cookbooks. As well as being presented as titbits at parties, they were commonly served at dinners – as a cold appetiser before the soup, or hot as the final course. As Hannah Maclurcan commented in 1898, 'A dinner or luncheon served without savouries, at the present time, would be worse than a dinner without vegetables. Gentlemen, as a rule, I think, prefer savouries any time to sweets'. Today whole books are devoted to the preparation of delicate morsels in the tradition of French hors d'oeuvres, Spanish tapas and Italian antipasto. These may indeed be served as appetisers, but a selection of such dishes also makes a perfect brunch, lunch or supper.

Recipes for home-made beverages also featured prominently in the manuscript and printed cookery books of last century, although many of the ingredients they called for – such as cowslips or clary – were unprocurable in the colonies. Even blackberries and nettles, popular for wine-making in England, were unknown here at that time, although both arrived soon enough and eventually overran the country. And some of the recipes were simply too time-consuming for the hard-working pioneers to attempt: who, for instance, would have had time to 'make ready the juice of 100 Seville oranges, which must first be pared very thin'? While cocktails really reached their heyday in the twentieth century, even as early as the 1860s Edward Abbott offered over eighty recipes for drinks, including a description of a most modern-sounding concoction, Blow My Skull, which as its name suggests was 'a remarkably powerful drink'.

ABOUT APPETISERS
An appetiser should make an immediate appeal to the eye and the palate, stimulating without satisfying the appetite. The French word *hors d'oeuvre* literally means 'outside of the principal work or main course'. Portions are small: when passed with drinks, they are bite-size; when served on a plate before dinner or at the table, a small plateful attractively arranged will suffice.

Australian Etiquette, 1960

Cheese Fingers

1/4 cup butter
3/4 cup flour
1/2 teaspoon baking powder

3/4 cup grated tasty cheese
salt and cayenne to taste
a little milk

Rub the butter into the flour, then mix in the baking powder, grated cheese and seasonings. Moisten with enough milk to make a stiff paste, then roll out and cut into fingers about 8 cm long and 2.5 cm wide. Bake on a tray in a hot oven for 5–10 minutes or until golden.

Cheese Crescents

250 g puff pastry
1 cup grated tasty cheese
1 tablespoon mustard

1/4 teaspoon cayenne
a little salt
beaten egg to glaze

Roll out the pastry and cut into rounds about 6 cm in diameter. Mix together the cheese, mustard, cayenne and salt and place a spoonful on each pastry round. Wet the edges, fold over and pinch together. Draw the ends together to form crescents, brush with egg and bake in a hot oven for about 10 minutes until puffed and golden.

Sardine Tablets

125 g shortcrust pastry
1 × 120 g can sardines in oil
4 hard-boiled eggs, chopped

2 tablespoons butter
1 teaspoon capers
salt and pepper

Roll out the pastry very thinly and use to line required number of patty tins. Fill with dry rice and bake blind. Meanwhile purée or blend the sardines with the hard-boiled eggs, butter, capers and a little pepper and salt. Fill the pastry cases with this mixture and bake in a hot oven for 5–10 minutes or until cooked through. Serve at once.

Sardine Twists

¹/₂ cup softened butter
¹/₂ cup cream cheese
1 cup flour
2 × 120 g cans sardines in
  oil, drained
1–2 tablespoons lemon juice
¹/₂ teaspoon curry powder
salt and pepper
2 hard-boiled eggs, finely
  chopped
2 tablespoons finely chopped
  parsley

Combine the butter and cream cheese, stirring until well blended. Mix in the flour, then knead for a few minutes and form into a ball. Refrigerate for 1 hour.

Mash the sardines with the lemon juice, curry powder, and salt and pepper to taste. Add eggs and parsley, and mix well. Roll out dough to about 10 mm thick. Cut into 10-cm squares and then cut these in half to form triangles. Chill until firm. Place 1 teaspoon of the filling in the centre of each triangle. Roll from the wide edge towards the point, twisting the ends to seal. Place on a tray and bake in a hot oven for about 10 minutes or until golden-brown.

Fish Balls

500 g white fish
4 slices wholemeal bread,
  crusts removed
¹/₂ cup milk
2 eggs
1 clove garlic, crushed
¹/₂ teaspoon cumin
¹/₂ teaspoon coriander
1 tablespoon finely chopped
  parsley
salt and pepper
¹/₂–1 cup oil

Poach the fish and then drain and flake into small pieces. Soak the bread in the milk, then squeeze dry and crumble between your fingers. Put everything except the oil into a large bowl and mix thoroughly, using your hands to knead the mixture until smooth. Form into 1-cm balls and sauté in hot oil until golden-brown on all sides. Drain well, and serve hot or cold.

ANCHOVY STRAWS

Take flour, butter, anchovy essence, cayenne, carmine, a little yolk of egg and cold water. Rub the butter into the flour; add the cayenne. Beat the yolk with the anchovy essence, carmine and a little water. Mix with the dry ingredients to a firm paste, roll out and cut into straws. Bake in a moderate–hot oven for about ten minutes and serve hot.

A CURE FOR HICCOUGH
One tablespoonful brown sugar moistened with pure vinegar.

A CURE FOR SCANDAL
Take of good nature 1 oz, of a herb called by the Indians 'mind-your-own-business' 1 oz. Mix this with a little charity for others, and two or three sprigs of discreet silence. Simmer all together in a vessel called circumspection for a short time and it will be ready for use.
The Green and Gold Cookery Book, 1928

Smoked-salmon Rolls

¹/₃ cup cream cheese

2 tablespoons lemon juice

1 tablespoon capers

2 teaspoons very finely chopped onion

1 teaspoon very finely chopped parsley

2 tablespoons mayonnaise

8 slices smoked salmon

Beat the cream cheese, lemon juice, capers, onion, parsley and mayonnaise until smooth. Spread some of the mixture on each slice of smoked salmon. Roll up, cover, and refrigerate.

Blue-cheese Dip

¹/₂ cup blue cheese (Roquefort or Castello)

3 tablespoons cream cheese

¹/₃ cup cream

pinch of cayenne

Mix the cheeses with the cream until smooth. Season to taste with cayenne, then chill.

Egg and Anchovy Mousse

8 anchovy fillets

a little milk

¹/₃ cup mayonnaise

2 tablespoons cream

2 tablespoons parsley

1 teaspoon anchovy essence (optional)

chilli sauce to taste

ground pepper to taste

4 hard-boiled eggs

1 egg white

Soak the anchovies in the milk for 10 minutes, then drain well. Blend the anchovies with the mayonnaise, cream, parsley, anchovy essence, chilli sauce and pepper. Add the hard-boiled eggs and beat well again. Taste, and adjust the seasonings. Whisk the egg white until stiff. Fold into the anchovy mixture, spoon into a serving dish, level the top, and refrigerate.

Olives on Toast

12 large olives

5 slices bread

1 tablespoon butter

$^1/_2$–1 cup grated tasty cheese

Remove the stones from the olives, keeping the flesh as whole as possible. Toast the bread, butter it, and then cut each slice into 4 rounds. Dip the buttered sides into the grated cheese, and also fill the olives with grated cheese. Place one olive on each round of toast, bake in a moderate oven until hot (about 5 minutes), then serve.

Birds' Nests

small triangles of stale bread

anchovy paste

shredded coconut

butter

salt

cayenne

Fry the bread, turning once, until browned on both sides. Drain on kitchen paper, spread with the anchovy paste and keep hot in the oven. Meanwhile, melt some butter in a pan, drop in the coconut and fry very slowly, turning frequently, until golden. Drain, dust with salt and cayenne, and pile on the prepared croutons. Serve hot or cold.

Chicken-liver Rolls

6 rashers bacon

6 chicken livers

pinch of cayenne

butter for frying (optional)

Cut each bacon rasher into pieces about 10 cm long. Cut each liver into 2 pieces, place one on each strip of bacon, and add a pinch of cayenne. Roll up, secure with a skewer, and fry in butter, grill, or bake in a hot oven. Serve at once.

CROÛTES À LA RUSSE

Fry round croûtons of bread, and when cold spread with caviare. Over that place a few very thin strips of marinaded herring and little piles of hard-boiled egg yolk (rubbed through a wire sieve). Place a small sprig of green chervil on top.

OLIVE MOUTHFULS

Whip a little cream. Season with salt, pepper, and anchovy sauce. Pile on to small round savoury biscuits. Top each with a small stuffed olive.

GRAPE JUICE

Take fresh, well-ripened, dark, juicy grapes, such as the Black Prince or Concords; pick from the stems, rejecting all that are imperfect; wash well, and put to cook in a saucepan with a pint of water for each three quarts of grapes. Cook slowly for half an hour, or until the grapes burst open; then drain off the juice through a jelly bag, filtering the skins and seeds through a separate bag. Reheat, add a very little white sugar if desired to have sweet, and can in jars the same as fruit; or, put in sterilised bottles, filling within an inch of the top, and cork at once with good, solid corks; cut off the corks close to the bottle, and seal over with sealing wax. Bottle the juice from the skins separately, as it will be less clear. Keep in a cool dark place, and do not move about unnecessarily.

A Friend in the Kitchen, 1918

HOP BEER

Ingredients: 20 litres rain water, ½ cup hops, ½ cup bruised ginger, 2 kg sugar, 2½ cups yeast, 1 tablespoon isinglass

Method: Boil the hops and ginger with the water for 20 minutes, stirring occasionally; then add the sugar, stir till dissolved, and take from the fire without letting it boil again. Strain into an open vessel, and leave till milk-warm; then add the yeast, cover with a thick woollen cloth, and let it work for 24 hours. In the mean time, soak the isinglass in 1 pint of cold water, and add to the beer at the end of 24 hours. This is to clear it. It will be ready to bottle next day, and will be fit for use in 2 days. The bottles must be perfectly dry.

Stuffed Mushrooms

12 medium, open mushrooms
1¼ cups dry breadcrumbs
½ cup chopped olives
6 anchovy fillets, chopped
2 tablespoons capers

3 tablespoons chopped parsley
2 teaspoons chopped thyme
⅓ cup olive oil
salt and pepper

Remove the stalks from the mushrooms. Combine
remaining ingredients thoroughly, stuff mushrooms with
mixture and bake in a moderate oven for 25 minutes.

Stuffed Nasturtium Flowers

½ cup cream cheese
1 tablespoon chopped capers
1 tablespoon chopped fresh
  herbs

freshly ground black pepper
12 nasturtium flowers

Combine the cream cheese, capers, herbs and pepper,
and spoon a little into the centre of each flower. Serve
on a platter lined with nasturtium leaves.

Smoked-trout Pâté

1 smoked trout, skinned and
  bones removed
150 ml thick sour cream (or
  crème fraîche)
1 tablespoon tomato paste

1 tablespoon sherry or brandy
1 tablespoon chopped fresh
  dill
black pepper

Purée everything together in a blender. When smooth
spoon into bowl and refrigerate for at least 2 hours.

HOME-MADE SYRUP FOR INDIGESTION

One shilling's worth essence
aniseed, 6 pennyworth
liquorice, 6 pennyworth bitter
aloes, 6 pennyworth gentian
root, as much cayenne pepper
as will lie on a 2/- piece. Put all
except the aniseed into a quart
of water and boil till dissolved.
Strain, and when cool add the
aniseed. Dose—One
teaspoonful in a wine-glass
of water.

MANDARIN'S CUP
Grate the rind of 3 oranges into a pint of water, add 3 tablespoonsful of sugar, boil gently for 5 minutes, add the juice of the 3 oranges and of 2 lemons. Let cool, add 1 pint tea which was strained directly after being infused, and a liqueur-glass of brandy. Ice before serving.

Summer Wine Cup

1 strip cucumber peel (about 10 cm long)
1 strip orange peel (about 10 cm long)
1 sprig borage
1 tablespoon sugar
3 tablespoons brandy
1 bottle dry white wine
1/2 cup soda water

Put the cucumber and orange peels, borage and sugar into a jug. Pour the brandy over and leave to stand for about 30 minutes. Add the white wine, soda water and 2 or 3 ice cubes.

Mulled Claret

1 bottle claret
1 cinnamon stick
6 cloves
2 tablespoons sugar
1 cup brandy
3 orange slices
3 lemon slices
ground nutmeg for serving

Combine all the ingredients except the nutmeg in a saucepan, and heat slowly (do not boil). Strain before serving hot in mugs, sprinkled with nutmeg.

Grandmother's Sherry Cocktail

1 bottle dry sherry
juice of 3 lemons
thinly peeled rind of 1 lemon
4 tablespoons sugar

Mix all the ingredients together and refrigerate for 48 hours. Strain before serving.

HOME-MADE WINES AND CORDIALS

You must not indulge in 'filthy beer', nor in porter, nor eat suppers—*the last are the devil to those who swallow dinner.*— BYRON TO MOORE, 1817.

Lord Palmerston (who as Minister has been accustomed to employ his pleasantries as PASSATONNERRES for troublesome visitors) one day related the following anecdote to a deputation of gentlemen, who waited on him to urge the reduction of the wine duties. Referring to the question of adulterations, 'I remember,' said his lordship, 'my grandfather, Lord Pembroke, when he placed wine before his guests, said, "There, gentlemen, is my champagne, my claret, &c. I am no great judge, and I give you this on the authority of my wine merchant; but I can answer for my port, for I made it myself".'

Now if Lord Palmerston had honoured us with his grandfather's mode for the manufacture of port, we should have been much obliged to him, for there is little doubt but that many home-made wines are infinitely superior to the foreign 'made up' for the English market, and from thence exported to the Australias . . . but as we have not been so fortunate as to obtain Lord Pembroke's recipe, we are obliged to have recourse to a few of our own.

Raspberry and Currant Wine.—Bruise three pints of fruit, and add one quart of water; let it stand, and after twenty-four hours strain the liquor, and put to every quart a pound of the best sugar. It will work of its own accord. Put a bottle of brandy to every five gallons; keep it for a time and bottle it.

Pink Champagne.—Dissolve nine pounds of loaf sugar over the fire in three gallons of water, remove the scum. Have ready picked a gallon of red and white currants, and pour over them the boiling liquor. Let it stand until cool, then add a tea-cupful of yeast; allow it to ferment for two days, then put it in a cask, and add some isinglass or white of egg to clear. Bung up the cask, but don't do this too soon, or there will be an explosion. When ready for bottling add a small lump of sugar to each bottle.

The English and Australian Cookery Book, 1861

Lemonade

6 lemons   *1 cup sugar*
6 cups water

Peel the rind from the lemons very thinly and place in
a saucepan with 2 cups of the water and the sugar.
Simmer for 5–10 minutes, then strain and cool. Squeeze
the juice from the lemons, strain into a jug, then add
the cooled syrup and the remaining water. Refrigerate
before serving.

Fruit Cocktail

2 cups puréed fresh fruit (e.g.   *juice of 2 oranges and 2*
*   berries, melon, mango,*   *   lemons*
*   banana, or a mixture)*   *soda or mineral water*
crushed ice

Spoon the puréed fruit over crushed ice in a jug. Add
orange and lemon juice and then top with soda or
mineral water.

AUSTRALIAN DRINK
Mix together 1 bottle
gingerbeer and 1 glass port
wine, and drink while
effervescing.

DOG'S NOSE
Warm half a pint of ale, and
add a wine-glassful of gin to it;
then add half a pint of cold ale,
and serve with toast.

*F*ROM THE LAND

Meat, Poultry and Game

IN THE ENGLISH TRADITION, meat was the staple of all three daily meals in nineteenth-century Australia. In cattle country, when a beast was killed the people of the homestead had fresh meat, chiefly steak, for three days and then corned beef for three weeks, for most of the carcase was cut up and placed in a cask of brine to preserve it. Veal was considered an expensive delicacy, and many cookery books make no mention at all of it. When it did appear in their pages it was usually as a dainty luncheon dish, often set in aspic and garnished elaborately.

Lamb and mutton account for most of the recipes in old books. As a Melbourne volume, published by Lothian in 1911, stated categorically, 'Mutton is undoubtedly the most popular meat in Australia'. Typical of the range of dishes made from each animal, wasting no part if possible, were Boiled Shanks, Sheep's Head Mould, Crumbed Sweetbreads or Brains, Boned Leg of Mutton, Haggis and even 'Australian Goose'.

While poultry generally signalled a special occasion, the pioneers ate an impressive range of native game. They were willing, it would seem, to try anything:

> A pleasant and grateful impression on my memory has a roasted porcupine, which I breakfasted on, on the top of a mountain near the Big Lagoon, in Tasmania, about five-and-thirty years ago; and if any epicure will hunt kangaroo on foot for two days fasting, and then try a roasted porcupine on a frosty morning, he will very likely have discovered a new pleasure.

For meats of any kind, the best of the old recipes are still firm favourites for their simplicity, economy and unfussy but fine flavours.

THE VICAR'S BEEF STEAK
Have the steak cut to a uniform thickness of not less than 1½ inches. Gash it with a sharp knife on both sides, making the cuts about ¼ inch deep and 2 inches apart, and place it in the following mixture for 4 or 5 hours: put into a deep dish a tablespoonful of brown vinegar, a tablespoonful of sugar, a saltspoonful of pepper, the same of salt, a tablespoonful of minced tarragon. The steak should be turned at frequent intervals during the time that it is in the marinade. When ready to cook the steak, drain it, dust it lightly with flour, and grill it over a very clear fire. When one side is done, turn it at once to cook the other. Serve as hot as possible with a piece of butter rubbed over the surface.

Carpet-bag à la Colchester

1 fillet steak per person, cut about 5 cm thick
3–4 raw oysters per steak
cayenne
lemon juice

Split the steak and fill it with the oysters, lightly seasoned with cayenne and lemon juice to taste. Sew up the steak and grill to the desired 'doneness'.

'Rubbing a steak over with oiled butter or salad oil prevents the juice escaping, and ensures it coming to table a rich brown outside and tender and juicy inside.'

Roast Sirloin or Ribs of Beef

2–3 kg sirloin of beef (bone left in) or rib roast
2–3 tablespoons butter
freshly ground black pepper
2 bay leaves, crumbled
6 tablespoons red wine
a little flour
1 cup beef stock

Preheat oven to hot. Smear beef with butter and sprinkle with pepper and crumbled bay leaves. Place beef on a rack in a roasting tin, bone ends down, and roast for 15 minutes. Reduce temperature to moderate and continue to cook, basting frequently with the wine. (Allow 15–18 minutes per 500 g for rare beef, 20–25 minutes per 500 g for medium and about 30 minutes per 500 g for well done). When cooked, season with salt and more pepper, remove to a serving platter and leave to stand in the open oven for 15 minutes before carving.

To make gravy, tip excess fat out of roasting pan and dust in a little flour to absorb the remaining juices, stirring in all the crusty bits. Add stock, season with salt and pepper, bring to the boil and simmer for a few minutes. Strain into a gravy boat.

Serve with Yorkshire Pudding (page 113).

A Great-grandmother's Recipe for Spiced Beef

2–3 kg topside or silverside of
  beef
³/₄ cup soft brown sugar
¹/₂ cup sea salt
1 tablespoon saltpetre

1 teaspoon cloves
1 tablespoon peppercorns
2 teaspoons allspice berries
1 tablespoon juniper berries

Rub the meat with the sugar and place in a deep earthenware or wooden tub. Leave for 12 hours, then crush spices and combine with the salt and saltpetre. Rub well into meat and leave in tub for 10 days, turning daily. When ready, rinse spices off meat and put it into a large pot with a little water. Cover tightly and simmer for 40 minutes per kilo.

Herb-crusted Lamb

2 racks of lamb (9 cutlets
  each)
1 cup fresh breadcrumbs
2 cloves garlic, chopped
1 onion, chopped
¹/₂ cup chopped parsley
1 teaspoon chopped fresh
  thyme

1 teaspoon chopped fresh
  marjoram
2 tablespoons grainy mustard
2 tablespoons olive oil
juice and grated rind of ¹/₂
  lemon

Combine breadcrumbs with garlic, onion, herbs, mustard, oil, and lemon juice and rind. Press onto back of each rack and refrigerate for at least 2 hours. Bake in a moderate oven for about 40 minutes.

There are particular joints which are reckoned more genteel for company than others—Sirloin of Beef, Quarter of Lamb, Haunch of Mutton, Chine of Doe or chine of Lamb if large enough for your party—or a very small round or edgebone of Beef.
Advice to a Young Lady in the Colonies, 1979

BASTINGS & DREDGINGS

The rarest ways of dressing of all manner of roast meats, either flesh or fowl, by sea and land, and divers ways of breading or dredging meats, to prevent the gravy from too much evaporating:

Dredgings

1 Flour mixed with grated bread.

2 Sweet herbs dried and powdered, and mixed with grated bread.

3 Lemon-peel dried, or orange-peel mixed with flour.

4 Sugar finely powdered, and mixed with pounded cinnamon and flour or grated bread.

5 Fennel seeds, corianders, cinnamon, and sugar, finely beaten and mixed with grated bread or flour.

6 For young pigs: grated bread or flour mixed with beaten nutmeg, ginger, pepper, sugar, and yolk of eggs.

7 Sugar, bread, and salt mixed.

Bastings

1 Fresh butter.

2 Clarified suet.

3 Minced sweet herbs, butter, and claret — especially for mutton and lamb.

4 Water and salt.

5 Cream and melted butter — especially for a flayed pig.

6 Yolk of eggs, grated biscuit, and juice of oranges.

The English and Australian Cookery Book, 1864

A Modern Pepperpot

1 teaspoon dark brown sugar
250 g oxtail, cut into pieces
500 g boneless pork or beef,
  cubed
1 kg chicken pieces
125 g salt beef, cubed
1/4 cup cassareep (or
  substitute 1/4 cup
  caramelised sugar)

1 onion, sliced
3 garlic cloves, chopped
2 red chillies, seeded and
  chopped
1 sprig thyme
salt

Put all the ingredients into a heavy casserole over a medium heat. Add water to cover, bring to boil, then reduce heat and simmer for 45 minutes. Allow to cool, then cover and refrigerate for at least 24 hours.

About 2 hours before it is to be served, remove casserole from the refrigerator and leave at room temperature for about 1 hour. Bake, covered, at 350°F for 1 hour. Serve with rice.

Liver and Onions

750 g onions, sliced
4 tablespoons oil
salt and pepper

400 g calf liver, sliced paper-
  thin

Simmer the onions gently with half the oil in a generous heavy frying-pan, covered at first so that some moisture is exuded. Cook until very soft and golden but not brown, then season with salt and pepper. To cook the liver, heat the remaining oil in a pan until sizzling. Add the liver pieces and stir for about half a minute, until liver is browning but still a little pink. Season, and serve at once on top of the onions in a warm serving dish.

A purée of apples, flavoured with a pinch of ground cloves, may be served instead of the onions.

PEPPER-POT WITH CASSAREEP

Have a wide-necked stone jar standing on the side of the stove furthest from the heat of the fire, put into it a sauce prepared as follows: Boil for an hour 1 quart of vinegar; 1/2 oz of ginger (green); 6 peppercorns; 2 chillies; 1 tablespoonful curry powder; 2 tablespoonfuls of chutney. Strain and put in a jar, then add as convenient any cold meat (cooked)—chops, steaks, scraps of chicken or game—any meat in fact. When you put in your scraps pour some cassareep sauce over each time. The pepper-pot should be served in its own pot with a table napkin round.

The Kookaburra Cookery Book, 1911

To Cook Cow-heel

Ingredients: Two cow-heels, a bunch of herbs, 1 carrot, 1 turnip, 1 onion, bread crumbs, dripping or butter. *Mode:* Having thoroughly cleaned the cow-heels, put them on to boil with the vegetables for about three hours, letting them do very slowly. When soft remove on to the board, and take out the bones. Now take a deep dish, lay the cow-heel upon it, with a little salt and pepper, cover with a layer of bread crumbs, put some little bits of butter over, pour about a cup of the soup round, and bake in a brisk oven till brown. This makes a nice luncheon dish cold.

The Antipodean Cookery Book, 1895

Tripe Fritters

1 cup dry breadcrumbs
1 teaspoon finely chopped
  fresh thyme
1 tablespoon finely grated
  parmesan

salt and pepper
500 g tripe
1 lemon, quartered
1/2 cup flour
1 egg yolk, beaten

Combine breadcrumbs in a bowl with the thyme, parmesan, salt and pepper. Cut tripe into strips about 10 cm long by 4 cm wide. Dry carefully, rub with lemon, coat with flour and brush with beaten yolk. Roll in the breadcrumb mixture and fry in oil until golden-brown.

Stewed Lamb Shanks

4 lamb shanks, cracked
1/4 cup flour
salt and pepper
2 tablespoons oil
1 clove garlic, chopped
2 onions, sliced
1 cup chopped celery
1/4 teaspoon salt
1 teaspoon sugar
pinch of cayenne

1 1/4 cups chicken or light beef
  stock
1 cup peeled and chopped
  tomatoes
1/2 cup white wine
1/4 teaspoon fresh rosemary
1/2 cup halved button
  mushrooms
chopped parsley

Dredge shanks in seasoned flour. Heat oil and sauté garlic, onions and celery until slightly softened. Add shanks and turn for a few minutes until lightly browned. Add salt, sugar, cayenne, stock, wine, rosemary and tomatoes, and simmer very gently, partly covered, for 1–1 1/2 hours or until meat is nearly falling off the bones. Add mushrooms and cook for a further 10 minutes. Serve sprinkled with parsley.

Mutton and Beans

500 g lean mutton or lamb,
  cut into 5-cm cubes
2 cups haricot beans, soaked
  overnight
1 tablespoon oil
1 onion, chopped
1 tablespoon flour

1 bay leaf
sprig of thyme
1 tablespoon tomato paste
2 cloves, garlic
salt and pepper
4 rashers bacon

Cook the haricot beans for 2 hours. When they are
nearly done, heat the oil in a pan and add the mutton
and onion. As the meat begins to brown, stir in flour,
and gradually add the water in which the beans were
cooked, plus the thyme, tomato paste, garlic, salt and
pepper. Continue to cook for 15 minutes. Put a layer of
the beans in a baking dish, cover with the mutton pieces
and then the rest of the beans. Pour the strained sauce
from the mutton over and top with the bacon. Bake,
uncovered, in a moderate oven for 1 hour.

Men, if they, as it is said they
do, prefer to dine at their clubs
and hotels, and arrange to be
from home on 'cold mutton'
days, show, we think, a very
laudable appreciation of what is
due to their own frames. We do
not think it would be in their
nature—exceptions are granted
to every rule—to go out to
dine, if they were sure of dining
comfortably and enjoyably at
home, and, if their 'cold
mutton' could be sometimes
metamorphosed into something
quite unrecognisable—lose its
identity in fact, and merge into
a tempting little dish really
appetising and inviting.
*The Housewife's Treasury of
Domestic Information*, n.d.

Oxtail Casserole

¹/₃ cup butter
2 oxtails, jointed
2 carrots, chopped
1 large onion, sliced
2 cloves garlic, chopped
small bouquet of herbs (thyme,
  bay leaf and parsley)

3 tablespoons brandy
pepper and salt
1 cup red wine
about 500 ml beef stock
juice and grated rind of 1
  orange
chopped parsley for garnish

Put butter in a large flame-proof casserole, add carrots,
onion, garlic and herbs, and cook until lightly browned.
Add the brandy and boil until reduced by half. Add
pepper and salt, wine and enough stock to cover and
then cook slowly, closely covered, in a low oven for
2 hours. Set aside until next day, remove all the fat, add
orange rind and juice and then reheat. Serve in the
casserole, garnished with finely chopped parsley.

In 1889, at the Universal Paris Exhibition, the composition of curry powder was set by decree: 34 g tamarind; 44 g onion; 20 g coriander; 5 g chilli pepper; 3 g turmeric; 2 g cumin; 3 g fenugreek; 2 g pepper; 2 g mustard.

The Colonel's Lamb Curry

1 kg shoulder of lamb, cubed
1 teaspoon ground ginger
1/4 teaspoon ground
  cinnamon
2 tablespoons oil
salt and pepper
extra 2 tablespoons oil
4 onions, sliced
2 cloves garlic, chopped

2 tablespoons curry powder
pinch of saffron
1 apple, grated
1 tablespoon raisins
1 tablespoon lemon juice or
  vinegar
1 cup water
3 tomatoes, peeled and
  chopped (optional)

Combine the ginger, cinnamon, oil, salt and pepper, rub into the lamb pieces and set aside for at least an hour. Heat the extra oil and fry the onion and garlic until lightly browned. Add the curry powder and lamb pieces and cook for a few minutes, stirring constantly. Add the remaining ingredients, including the tomatoes if used (in which case less water will be needed), cover and cook gently for 45 minutes or until meat is tender and gravy has thickened. Serve with hot boiled rice and a selection of chutneys.

A Dish of Lamb Kidneys

2–3 lamb kidneys per person
2 rashers bacon per person
1/2–1 cup flour

salt and pepper
water

Trim the kidneys and cut each into about 8 pieces. Cut bacon into 2-cm squares. Dredge kidneys in seasoned flour, shaking to remove any excess. Place kidneys and bacon in medium saucepan and add water almost to cover. Bring gradually to a simmer and cook very gently for about 30 minutes or until kidneys are tender and gravy has thickened slightly and turned a rich pink. (Do not let the mixture boil, as this can cause the kidneys to become tough.) Serve on triangles of hot buttered toast.

Blanquette de Veau

2 tablespoons butter
750 g veal, cut into neat
  pieces
2¹/₂ cups chicken or
  light beef stock
1 extra tablespoon butter

¹/₄ cup flour
2 egg yolks
¹/₂ cup cream
1 teaspoon lemon juice
salt and pepper

Melt the butter in a pan and seal veal pieces on all sides without browning. Add the stock and then simmer until tender. Melt the butter in a medium saucepan and stir in the flour. Gradually add the strained stock (reserving the veal pieces), stirring to remove any lumps, and then simmer for 10 minutes. Stir the egg yolks into the cream and pour into the sauce. Cook a few minutes (do not let boil), then add the veal, lemon juice, salt and pepper. Serve in a deep dish.

Pork Chops with Mustard Sauce

4 pork chops
¹/₄ cup flour
salt and pepper
a little oil
³/₄ cup cream

1 tablespoon French mustard
¹/₄ cup white wine
a little chopped fresh thyme
2 tablespoons chopped parsley

Dredge chops in flour mixed with salt and pepper. Heat oil in a frying pan and sauté chops on both sides until lightly browned and cooked through. Drain and keep warm on a serving dish. Stir mustard into the pan juices, add wine, cream, salt, pepper and thyme, stirring in any crusty bits stuck to the bottom of the pan. Simmer gently until slightly thickened, then spoon over chops. Garnish with finely chopped parsley.

Give an Englishman a pound of meat: the chances are, that two to one, he rushes to the frying-pan, and frizzles all the goodness out of it. How different the Frenchman proceeds: he has recourse to the *pot au feu*, and, with the assistance of every kind of vegetable that he can lay his hands on, he will have ready, in a few hours, the most savoury of dishes, and the most digestible; hence the common saying, 'as many Frenchmen, as many cooks'.
The English and Australian Cookery Book, 1864

MEATS
Meat-eating tends to excite the
passions. This is seen in the
animal kingdom. The animals
that are mild, patient and docile
are generally herbivorous, such
as the cow, the sheep, the horse;
while the excitable, quick
tempered, and ferocious
animals are meat eaters, such as
the lion, the tiger, the leopard.
A meat diet also tends to
constipation, the great scourge
of the race.

A Friend in the Kitchen, 1918

'Australian Goose'

½ cup soft breadcrumbs
a few sage leaves
1 onion
2 rashers bacon, chopped
salt and pepper
1 egg
3 pork fillets

½ cup flour
extra salt and pepper
1 tablespoon butter
1 carrot, sliced
1–2 cups light stock
chopped parsley

Combine breadcrumbs, sage, half of the onion
(chopped), bacon, salt, pepper and egg. Cut a pocket in
each pork fillet and insert breadcrumb mixture. Cut in
half, tie round and then roll in flour, salt and pepper.
Heat butter in a frying pan, brown the pork rolls, and
drain. In a buttered pie dish place the carrot, remainder
of the onion (sliced), then a sprinkling of pepper and
salt. Lay the pork on top and cover with stock. Cover
dish with foil and bake in a moderate oven for 1 hour.
Lift out meat, remove string, arrange in a hot dish. Rub
the cooking liquid through a sieve, remove fat and then
pour sauce over the meat. Garnish with parsley.

'The stuffing mixture may also be used to farce a leg
of mutton, in which you have made an incision at the
shank end. Fasten with a skewer and bake as usual.' This
version was often also known as Poor Man's Goose.

SAUSAGES

If the reader is wise he will always abstain from eating sausages, unless he knows of their manufacture, should he not be desirous of partaking of the man who, Dickens cleverly informs us, was chopped into sausage meat, and all that remained of him was his buttons. It is a positive and notorious fact in all parts of the world, that every kind of unwholesome meat is minced into sausages. Who would ever think of putting good meat into sausages when the mince and sage will effectively smother the flavour of putrid stuff? We now give a few modern ways of making at home a very favourite relish, with the aid of a twenty-five shilling machine.

Sausages: to each pound of pork allow a pound of veal and one pound of fat—that is, two parts lean to one part of fat. Mix them well, and allow a pound of bread-crumbs, thyme, parsley, an ounce of sage, two heads of leeks, a little garlic or a shalot, chopped fine, with pepper, salt, and nutmeg. To each pound allow one egg, the yolks and whites separate; beat both well, mix in the yolks, and as much of the whites as necessary to moisten the bread, and add all the ingredients together.

Worcester Sausages are made of beef, suet, and allspice, with other herbs.

Mutton Sausages: to each pound of mutton add a pound of beef suet, and anchovies, for relish, chopped fine, and what seasoning you choose. Herbs or not, as you please.

Veal Sausages: veal sausages are made like Oxford sausages, except bacon is used instead of sage.

Savoury Sausages: salt a piece of lean beef and pork with common salt, a little saltpetre, sugar, black pepper, and allspice, for two days. Season with pepper, cayenne, garlic, and a shalot; and mince fine and put into clean gut. Smoke them. When wanted for use they may be boiled and eaten cold.

The English and Australian Cookery Book, 1864

Dorset Rabbit

1 young rabbit, cut into
  serving pieces
1/2 cup flour
salt and pepper
2 tablespoons chopped fresh
  sage
1/2 cup milk

3 rashers bacon, chopped
4 onions, chopped
1/4 cup butter
1 cup fresh breadcrumbs
grated rind of 1/2 lemon
2 tablespoons chopped parsley
1 egg

Dredge the rabbit pieces in the flour, shaking to remove any excess. Place in a deep ovenproof dish and sprinkle with salt, pepper and sage. Pour the milk over, then scatter the bacon on top. Sauté the onions in the butter until lightly golden, allow to cool a little and then mix with the breadcrumbs, lemon rind and parsley. Bind this mixture with the beaten egg, then spread over the rabbit and bake in a low oven for 1½–2 hours or until rabbit is tender and the crust is browned.

Chicken Cutlets

4 chicken breast fillets
2 cups chicken stock
4–6 tablespoons foie gras or
  liverwurst
2 eggs, beaten
2 cups dry breadcrumbs

4 tablespoons butter
1 cup thickened cream
salt and pepper
2 tablespoons chopped fresh
  herbs

Poach the chicken breasts in the stock until tender and allow to cool (reserve 1/2 cup of the stock). Slice each through into 2 neat pieces, spread the foie gras between and sandwich together. Dip in egg and crumbs and fry in the butter until golden-brown on both sides. Serve with a rich sauce made of the cream heated with 1/2 cup of the stock, salt and pepper, and the chopped herbs (chives, parsley or tarragon).

ROAST PIGMY GOOSE
The pigmy goose is a very small bird, but without doubt one of the sweetest of the Australian birds, and rather rare. Wash inside and out, prepare for stuffing. Sprinkle with pepper and salt, and rub a little flour over them. Stuffing—Allow about six oysters to each bird, soak the bread in a little milk, squeeze it out on to a plate, put in a teaspoonful of chopped parsley, the yolk of one egg and a teaspoonful of butter, divide it equally for as many birds as you have, and to each part add six oysters, pepper and salt. When the birds are stuffed, lay them on a baking dish and cover with buttered paper, bake in a quick oven. Serve on toast.
Mrs Maclurcan's Cookery Book, 1898

Devilled Poultry

1 tablespoon French mustard
1 tablespoon mango chutney
1 teaspoon Worcestershire sauce (or 1 teaspoon curry powder)
2 tablespoons softened butter
pinch of salt
$^{1}/_{4}$ teaspoon cayenne
750 g cooked chicken, duck or turkey, pulled apart into largish pieces
1 cup dry breadcrumbs
juice of 1 lemon
2 tablespoons chopped parsley

Combine the first six ingredients. Slash the poultry pieces with a knife and spread with the devil mixture, pressing in well with your fingers. Leave for a few hours or overnight. Just before serving, sprinkle with the breadcrumbs, put under a hot griller or in a hot oven, and cook until crusty and golden. Serve on a bed of watercress, garnished with lemon juice and chopped parsley. A jug of hot cream soured with a little vinegar or lemon juice may be handed separately.

Chicken Baked in Salt

1 medium chicken
1.5 kg coarse sea salt
2 tablespoons oil or melted butter
pepper
sprig of thyme
$^{1}/_{2}$ lemon, sliced

Put about one-third of the salt into a deep casserole. Brush the chicken with the oil or butter, and sprinkle with pepper. Put the thyme and lemon into the chicken's cavity and wrap loosely in greaseproof paper. Place on top of the salt in the casserole and then pour the rest around it to cover completely. Cover, and bake in a moderate–hot oven for $1^{1}/_{2}$ hours. Before serving, break the salt crust, remove and unwrap the chicken, and serve on a heated platter.

Chicken en Cocotte

2 tablespoons butter
2 onions, chopped
6 mushrooms, chopped
2 chicken livers, chopped
2 rashers bacon, cut into
  largish squares
1 medium chicken

6 medium potatoes, thinly
  sliced
6 artichoke hearts, halved
1 cup chicken stock
$^{1}/_{2}$ cup white wine
salt and pepper

Heat the butter and sauté the onions gently until golden. Add the mushrooms, cook for 5 minutes, then add the chicken livers, mixing well, and cook for a further minute or two. Stuff the chicken with this mixture. Put the bacon into a flame-proof casserole over a gentle heat until the fat begins to run, then turn up the heat a little and let the bacon brown. Remove the bacon, then put in the chicken and brown on all sides. Return the bacon to the pan and surround the chicken with the sliced potatoes and the artichoke hearts, and cook uncovered in a moderate oven for 1 hour. Remove the chicken and vegetables from the pot, pour in the stock and wine and boil over a moderate heat to reduce by about half. Season with salt and pepper, return chicken and vegetables to the pot, and serve.

Roast Quail

Truss 4 quail and wrap each in a rasher of bacon. Put a tablespoon or two of butter in a baking dish and roast the quail in a moderate oven for 15 minutes, basting well. Serve on triangles of fried bread, garnished with watercress. Bread Sauce (page 107) is a traditional accompaniment.

A DELICIOUS WAY TO COOK A FOWL

Take a fowl, stuff it with a mixture of oysters, breadcrumbs and butter seasoning mixed with a little cream, place fowl in a stewpan with a small piece of butter, the liquor from oysters, pepper and salt, cover well, and stand pan in another of boiling water, steam for an hour or longer, according to the age of fowl. Serve with rich oyster sauce poured over. Serve very hot.

CLEANING AND PREPARING GROUND GAME

By ground game I mean wallaby, bandicoot, paddy-melon, iguana, etc., etc. There is no more distasteful office for a lady to have to do than this, and though my way may be no better than any other, I offer it for the sake of those inexperienced housewives who may have often thrown away good food rather than go through the ordeal of preparing it for cooking. In the first place, none of these animals should be hung up uncleaned; like fish, they require to be cleaned at once.

About the skinning I need say little, as that is very simple, merely advising the use of a sharp penknife. Having skinned it, take a bucket of water, and with the wallaby, or whatever it may be, seek a place some short distance from the house. I advise this on account of the strong smell, as well as the mess you thus avoid making in the kitchen. Make a cut from the neck to the vent, cut across where the inside is attached top and bottom, and then you can easily tear the whole of the inside out.

Plunge the carcass into the water, and wash it well, when it is ready to be taken back to the kitchen, and cut up on the meat board. A large wallaby or kangaroo requires to be dressed just the same as a sheep, but that work is usually done by the men folk of the household.

All Australian ground game has a strong peculiar flavour, which many people dislike. It can be done away with to a great extent by soaking in vinegar and water, or by burying for several hours . . .

The iguana is little or no trouble to prepare, and the tail part is that most generally used. It should be skinned, parboiled, and used for curry, or many Bushmen like it cooked on the ashes, particularly if the iguana be a young one. For my own part, I know of nothing we have in the Bush in the way of animal food that is so appetising as the tail of a young iguana cooked black's fashion on the ashes.

The Antipodean Cookery Book, 1895

Kangaroo Pie

2 cups red wine

1 clove garlic, finely chopped

3 cloves

4 juniper berries

4 allspice berries

1 sprig each of thyme and
    rosemary

2 bay leaves

750 g kangaroo fillets, cut
    into 5-cm pieces

1¹/₂ cups flour

salt and pepper

250 g bacon, cubed

2 onions, chopped

1 cup canned tomatoes,
    drained

2 tablespoons chopped parsley

500 g flaky pastry

Combine the first seven ingredients and marinate the
kangaroo pieces for at least 24 hours (preferably
longer). Drain the meat (reserve the marinade), then
dry and dredge in seasoned flour. Heat oil in a pan,
sauté the meat until golden and then place in a large
casserole. Sauté the bacon and onions in the same pan,
then pour over the kangaroo fillets. Add the marinade,
tomatoes and parsley, and bake, covered, in a slow oven
for about 1 hour or until tender. Allow to cool. Line a
pie dish with half the pastry, fill with the casserole
mixture, top with the remaining pastry and bake for
35–45 minutes or until golden-brown.

Roast Emeu

This is very unctuous sort of
food, and much resembles
coarse beef in flavour. At the
early establishment of the
colony it was generally partaken
of, but we cannot recommend it
to the epicure, unless he has the
sailor's digestion elsewhere
alluded to. In the first
settlement of Hobart Town,
and, we believe, Sydney,
kangaroo was purchased into
the public stores at a shilling a
pound, and served out to the
only two classes of inhabitants—
the military and the bond—
then in being, with a few
officers. Emeu can either be
roasted or boiled.

*The English and Australian
Cookery Book*, 1864

FROM THE WATERS

Fish and Other Seafood

EDWARD ABBOTT, in his book of 1864, dealt at great length with fish, listing the varieties found in each state and giving the correct way of cooking each one. Other early cookery books divided fish into groups according to their flesh type. The most highly prized were white fish – whiting, rock cod, Murray cod and flathead – as in these the fat or oil is in the liver and the rest of the flesh is firm and white. They recommended that fish with oily flesh be boiled whole, and suggested that the housewife place a square of clean muslin under the fish, with the four corners protruding out of the saucepan, so that when it was cooked the fish could be removed easily and then as easily lowered on to a large dish. There were numerous recipes for sauces to serve with fish, and it was often suggested that a bunch of parsley be placed on the head, 'which sometimes looks unsightly'. A fish could be further decorated with butterflies, the body made of parsley stem, and the two wings cut from thin slices of lemon.

Many books gave detailed instructions for choosing fish at the market, and for keeping oysters fresh until required: they should be put in a tub with salted water and a handful of oatmeal, left undisturbed for 12 hours, then drained and left to stand for another 12 hours, the whole process being repeated again. The reader was assured that 'oysters are fattened very much by this treatment'. Very sensibly, books intended for use in country areas devoted many pages to meals based around tinned fish, originally sardines and later salmon. Tuna was not yet widely available, but tinned whitebait was immensely popular and for those who could not afford this expensive luxury there were recipes for 'mock whitebait' made from thin slivers of mullet.

BOUILLABAISSE
Thackeray's "Ballad of
Bouillabaisse" has made this
fish soup famous to English-
speaking peoples, and
Australians going to England
can sample it en route in its
Provençal home, Marseilles.
Sometimes the soup is strained
and served separately from the
fish, which is served in another
dish, then sippets of toast are
served with the soup. But in
Marseilles it is served all
together.

Seafood Stew

4 tablespoons oil	1 tablespoon chopped parsley
2 onions, sliced	1/2 teaspoon saffron
2 cloves	salt and pepper
2 bay leaves	4 cups water or fish stock
2 leeks, sliced	1/2 cup white wine
2 cloves garlic, chopped	1 kg mixed fish
2 medium tomatoes, peeled	rind of 1 orange and
and chopped	1 lemon, thinly sliced

Heat the oil in a pot, add the onions, cloves, bay leaves,
leeks, garlic, tomatoes, parsley, saffron, salt and pepper.
Simmer until onion is transparent, then add white wine,
fish, and stock or water and simmer for 20 minutes. Add
orange and lemon rind a few minutes before serving.

Creamy Smoked Fish

1 kg smoked fish	1 cup cream
1 1/2 cups milk	salt and pepper
1 1/2 cups water	pinch of ground turmeric or
1 bay leaf	saffron
2 tablespoons butter	1 tablespoon finely chopped
2 tablespoons flour	parsley

Place fish in a saucepan, add milk, water and bay leaf,
and bring slowly to the boil. Remove from heat and
leave to stand for 30 minutes or so, then strain,
reserving the liquid. In a fresh saucepan melt the butter
and stir in the flour.

Gradually add 1 1/2 cups of the cooking liquid, stirring
constantly until mixture begins to thicken. Add cream,
salt, pepper and turmeric or saffron, and continue to
cook gently for a few more minutes. Flake fish into
largish pieces, add to sauce and heat again, adding a
little more cream or cooking liquid if sauce is too thick.
Serve garnished with chopped parsley and accompanied
by triangles of crisp toast.

Mussels and Beer

2 tablespoons butter
1 onion, chopped
1 clove garlic, chopped
1 cup beer
sprig of thyme
2 tablespoons chopped parsley

1 bay leaf
1 kg mussels, scrubbed
1/2 cup cream
salt and pepper
chopped parsley and chives
for garnish

Heat butter in a good-sized pot, add onion and garlic, and cook until onion is transparent. Add beer, thyme, parsley and bay leaf, and simmer for 5 minutes. Place mussels in the pot, cover and steam for a few minutes or until shells open. Remove mussels to a warm serving dish, transfer cooking liquor to a small saucepan and boil for 5 minutes or until reduced a little. Add cream, and salt and pepper to taste, and heat through. Serve mussels with sauce poured over, garnished with chopped parsley and chives.

Cornish Baked Mackerel

4 medium mackerel,
  heads and tails removed
1/2 cup butter
1/2 cup white wine
2 teaspooons vinegar

pinch of cayenne
salt and pepper
2 tablespoons flour
3/4 cup dry breadcrumbs

Grease a shallow ovenproof dish with 2 tablespoons of the butter. Put in the mackerel, mix the wine, vinegar, cayenne, salt and pepper and pour over the fish. Mash 1/4 cup of the butter with the flour and divide in 4, pressing one piece onto each fish. Cover with foil and bake in a moderate oven for 15 minutes. Remove the foil, scatter the breadcrumbs over the fish, dot with the remaining butter and bake for a further 15 minutes until the top is golden.

A FISHERMAN'S RECIPE
FOR COOKING GARFISH
Split the fish right down to the
tail and open well out, so that
when placed rib bones down,
the latter rest flat on the pan. In
the pan use a very little lard, oil,
or butter.

If fried on this side only, until
becomes a light-brown colour,
the bones will be found to be
fried up, and the flavour of the
fish will be greatly improved.
Serve very hot with fried
parsley.

Fillets of Whiting
à la Gahreemai

4 whiting fillets	$^1/_2$ cup white wine
2 tablespoons melted butter	$^1/_2$ cup water
salt and pepper	
$^1/_4$ cup orange juice	ORANGE SALAD
1 tablespoon finely chopped	3 oranges
orange rind	1 dessertspoon tarragon
2 tablespoons finely chopped	vinegar
capers or olives	2 tablespoons olive oil
1 tablespoon finely chopped	salt and pepper
parsley	1 tablespoon chopped fresh
pinch of paprika	basil

Brush the fillets with the butter, season with salt and
pepper, then sprinkle with the orange juice and rind
and the capers or olives. Roll up the fillets tightly, pack
into a greased pie dish, sprinkle with parsley and
paprika, and pour the wine and water over. Place
buttered foil on top and cook in a moderate oven for
8–10 minutes. Garnish with slices of orange and serve
with the orange salad.

Peel the oranges, slice very thinly and lay slightly
overlapping on a flat dish. Combine the tarragon
vinegar, oil, salt and pepper, and drizzle over orange
slices. Garnish with chopped basil.

Fish Fillets with Champagne Sauce

500 g flounder or John Dory
  fillets
1 small onion, chopped
1 bay leaf
sprig of parsley
³/₄ cup white wine
¹/₂ cup water
salt and pepper

CHAMPAGNE SAUCE
1 tablespoon butter
1 onion, chopped
1 cup champagne
1 cup cream
2 tablespoons chopped dill or
  tarragon
1 tablespoon finely chopped
  parsley

Butter an ovenproof dish and put in fish fillets in one layer. Sprinkle with the chopped onion and add the bay leaf, parsley, wine, water, and salt and pepper. Cover dish with foil and cook in a moderate oven for about 15 minutes or until flesh flakes easily. Remove fish and keep warm in the oven. Strain the liquid and reserve 3 tablespoons to flavour the sauce.

To make the sauce, melt the butter in a saucepan, add the chopped onion and cook for a few minutes until softened. Add the champagne and reserved cooking liquid, and boil until reduced by half (about 10 minutes). Remove from heat, stir in the cream and simmer until sauce begins to thicken. Add the herbs just before serving.

How to Cook Husbands

A great many husbands are spoiled by mismanagement. Some women go about as if their husbands were bladders, and blow them up; others let them freeze by their carelessness and indifference. Some keep them in a stew, by irritating ways and words; others roast them; some keep them in pickle all their lives. Now, it is not to be supposed that any husband will be good, managed in this way—turnips wouldn't, onions wouldn't, cabbage heads wouldn't, and husbands won't.

In selecting your husband you should not be guided by the silvery appearance as in buying mackerel, or by the golden tint as if you wanted salmon. Be sure to select him yourself, as tastes differ. And by the way, don't go to market for him, as the best are always brought to your door.

Tie him in the kettle with a strong cord called 'comfort', as the one called 'duty' is apt to be weak. Make a clear, strong, steady fire out of love, neatness, and cheerfulness. Set him as near this as seems to agree with him. If he sputters and frizzles, don't be anxious; some husbands do this till they are quite done. Add a little sugar, in the form of what confectioners call kisses, but no vinegar or pepper on any account. A little spice improves them, but it must be used with judgment. Don't stick any sharp instrument into him to see if he is becoming tender. Stir him gently, watching the while lest he should lie too close to the kettle and so be inert and useless.

When properly treated they are really delicious.

The Green and Gold Cookery Book, 1928

Hint

Cooks generally, after frying fish, throw away the fat—an extravagance to be reprehended. A knife applied to fish is likely to spoil the delicacy of its flavour; so that it should be helped with a silver slice or trowel, and be eaten with a silver fork and bread, or a fish-knife. Fried fish should never be sent to table covered, because the steam that rises is condensed by the cover, and falls back on the fish, which thereby becomes soddened, and loses its crispness and flavour. Boiled fish is improved by a little vinegar being put into the water, an onion, and a few sweet herbs.

The English and Australian Cookery Book, 1864

Marinated Trout

1 tablespoon rock salt

1 tablespoon sugar

1 heaped teaspoon crushed
 peppercorns

2 large trout fillets (about
 750 g)

2 tablespoons chopped fresh
 dill

MUSTARD MAYONNAISE

1 egg yolk

2 tablespoons French mustard

1/2 teaspoon sugar

1 tablespoon wine vinegar

6 tablespoons oil

salt and pepper

1 tablespoon chopped fresh
 dill

Combine salt, sugar and peppercorns. Take a sheet of
foil large enough to wrap the fillets, sprinkle one-third
of the salt mixture over and then cover with one-third of
the dill. Place one trout fillet, skin down, over the dill,
cover with another third of the salt mixture and dill,
then repeat with remaining ingredients, rubbing
mixture in well. Wrap trout firmly in the foil and weight
down with two or three cans.

Refrigerate for at least 24 hours (no longer than
4 days), turning trout several times. Remove from foil,
scrape off seasonings and cut into slices. Serve with
brown bread and butter and Mustard Mayonnaise.

To make the Mustard Mayonnaise, beat the egg yolk
with the mustard and sugar until smooth. Stir in the
vinegar, then gradually add the oil, beating constantly,
until mixture thickens. Season with salt and pepper to
taste and add the chopped dill. Refrigerate before
serving.

CAVICHED FISH

Any small cold fish, put in a
deep dish, cover with nicely
browned onion, whole spice,
peppercorns, allspice, salt to
taste. Cover with hot vinegar
and leave a few days before
eating.

CRAYFISH

Boil, in a pint of milk, two blades of mace, one onion, sliced, cayenne, and salt, with lemon, a little butter and flour, and a gill of cream, and serve with crayfish.

This was considered a *recherché* dish at a mayor's feast in Tasmania.

The English and Australian Cookery Book, 1864

Trout in Paper

4 small trout or mullet
salt and pepper
1 teaspoon crushed garlic
4 tablespoons chopped fresh
  herbs (chervil, parsley and
  chives)

4 tablespoons butter
4 tablespoons fresh
  breadcrumbs
4 tablespoons vermouth or
  white wine

Make one or two diagonal slashes across the thickest part of the fish. Place each on a largish piece of buttered foil, season with salt and pepper, and sprinkle a quarter of the garlic and chopped herbs over each. Spoon some of the breadcrumbs (to soak up the juices) and butter into the cavity of each fish and splash the vermouth or wine over before sealing the package. Bake in a moderate oven for 15–20 minutes or until flesh flakes. Serve in the parcels, with lemon wedges handed separately.

Old-fashioned Fish Pie

500 g cooked white fish
6 mushrooms, chopped
1 tablespoon butter
1 tablespoon flour
1¼ cups milk
salt and pepper

6 oysters, halved (optional)
1 tablespoon chopped parsley
juice of 1 lemon
1–1½ cups fresh
  breadcrumbs
extra butter for baking

Remove the skin and bones from the fish, flake flesh finely and mix with the mushrooms. Melt the butter in a pan, stir in the flour and then add the milk gradually and simmer until sauce has thickened slightly. Mix in the fish and mushrooms, season with salt and pepper to taste, then add the oysters and parsley. Grease a pie dish, pour in the mixture, sprinkle the lemon juice over and scatter with breadcrumbs. Dot with the extra butter and bake in a moderate–hot oven for about 20 minutes or until top has browned.

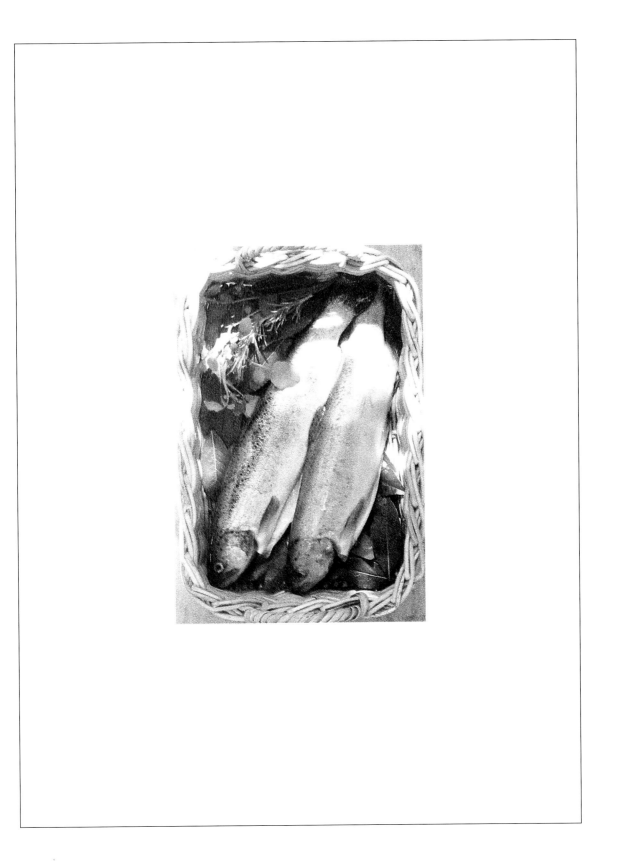

ON FISH

We grow tired of saying, and of hearing it said, that fish is not nearly enough used in this country; and of the truism that we eat too much meat, and that if we ate more fish we would be better off in body and pocket. We say these things over and over again, and we get no further. We have garfish or mullet occasionally; we use a tin of fish when at a loss for something to help out. Now and again we buy some blue cod, smoked barracouta, or ling; but, in the ordinary small villa and cottage, fish is looked upon as rather a nuisance, and in many homes is seen very rarely indeed. Nearly everyone fries fish, and if it is properly done it is excellent; when it is badly fried it is horrid. The same thing may be said of boiled fish. In one case, if the cook is careless, the fish appears limp, sodden, burnt in some places, not cooked in others. In the other case it will have water oozing from it, and lie in an ungainly heap on the dish. For these reasons, if the cook has not learnt to cook fish, or will not try, fried and boiled fish are best avoided.

The Melbourne Cookery Book, c. 1900

ROAST TASMANIAN SALMON

Pour 4 tablespoons olive oil into a heavy oven pan and put in a hot oven for a minute or two. Place 4 thick Tasmanian salmon steaks in the pan and bake, also in a hot oven, for about 3 minutes a side or until flesh flakes when tested. Serve at once with Mustard Butter, made as follows: beat 250 g butter until soft, then stir in 2 tablespoons of finely chopped parsley, 2 teaspoons of French mustard, lemon juice to taste, a generous pinch of cayenne, and white pepper. Roll into a cylinder, chill, and cut into thickish slices to serve.

Salad of Yabbies

1 kg yabbies
2 litres water or fish stock
1¹/₂ cups mayonnaise

2 tablespoons chopped fresh
 tarragon or dill
1 bunch watercress

Bring water or stock to the boil and drop in the yabbies.
Simmer for about 5 minutes or until shells turn red.
Remove from pot, separate tails from heads, cut tails in
half lengthways and remove flesh. Stir the tarragon or
dill into the mayonnaise and toss yabbies through while
still warm. Serve on a bed of watercress.

Scallops in a Curry Cream

750 g scallops
1 cup white wine
1 bay leaf
2 tablespoons butter

¹/₂ teaspoon curry powder
1¹/₄ cups cream
2 egg yolks, beaten
salt and pepper

Slice the scallops into two rounds and set aside the
orange coral. Simmer the white parts in the wine with
the bay leaf for a few minutes only, then drain (keep the
cooking liquid). Heat the butter, add curry powder and
scallops and sauté for 3–4 minutes. Remove scallops
with a slotted spoon and keep warm in the oven. Pour
the wine onto the butter and curry powder, stir well and
boil to reduce by about half. Stir in the cream, salt and
pepper, and boil hard again for about 5 minutes.
Remove from the heat and stir in the beaten egg yolks
and the scallops (plus the coral). Cook *very* gently for
2–3 minutes or until sauce is beginning to thicken.
Serve with boiled rice or small new potatoes.

SALMON LAST CENTURY
The Colonial salmon, and the
English fish of that name—the
Salmo salar of Linnæus—are
dissimilar in every possible
respect. The Australian colonists
have been endeavouring to
procure the latter from the
mother country for some time
past. At the last meeting of the
Acclimatisation Society, at
Melbourne, the Governor, Sir
Charles Darling, in the chair,
the Council stated that the
salmon claimed priority of
notice, as it occupied the
anxious attention, and as many
previous difficulties were now
removed by the experiments
carried out successfully in
London by the friends of
acclimatisation, it may be
confidently expected that before
many months have passed
Tasmanian waters will receive
the first promised supply of
British fish.
*The English and Australian
Cookery Book*, 1864

Vegetable Dishes

OLD COOKERY MANUALS gave recipes for only a limited number of vegetables, and all too often their instructions were as follows: 'Boil in a saucepan full of well-salted water until thoroughly done'; sometimes the cook was advised to add a good pinch of soda as well.

In the English tradition, vegetables were seen chiefly as an accompaniment to meat and on this matter *The Kingswood Cookery Book* made its opinion plain:

> Australian housekeepers are often worried, I think, about vegetables, and long for some change from cabbages and beans, which appear with such regularity on the dinner table. Foreigners all profess to dislike our vegetables boiled plainly in water, and say very unpleasant things about English cooks in consequence. But, laugh at us as they may, plainly-boiled vegetables are by far the best, if they are served *with* the roast beef of old England. Dressed vegetables are very nice as a separate course, but *with* roast meat for English tastes there is nothing like plain, well-cooked vegetables . . .

Today we tend to eat our vegetables raw, lightly steamed, or stir-fried, and often as a course or a meal on their own. A modern chef's advice to someone about to drop peeled vegetables into boiling salted water might well be the same as Mr Punch's recommendation to those about to marry – 'Don't!'. Happily, from time to time between the 'Baked', 'Boiled' and 'Creamed' dishes of early cookery books one can find some quite enlightened vegetable recipes.

Scalloped Jerusalem Artichokes

500 g Jerusalem artichokes
1 tablespoon butter
1 tablespoon flour
1 cup cream
1/2 teaspoon anchovy paste

1 egg yolk
a little lemon juice
salt and pepper
pinch of cayenne
1/2 cup breadcrumbs

Cook the artichokes until tender and then cut them into medium pieces. Melt the butter in a pan and add the flour, stirring until smooth. Add the cream and anchovy paste, remove from heat and then add the egg yolk, lemon juice to taste, salt, pepper and cayenne. Stir the artichokes into this sauce and pour into a gratin dish. Sprinkle the top with breadcrumbs, dot with butter and bake in a moderate oven for about 15 minutes.

'Remains of celery or cauliflower can be cooked in the same way.'

Asparagus with Eggs

24 asparagus spears
4 eggs

1 cup melted butter
salt and pepper

Trim off the woody ends of the asparagus stalks. Cook upright (heads exposed), in a pan of boiling salted water for about 10 minutes or until just tender, then drain and keep warm on a heated serving plate. Put the eggs in boiling water to cover and bring water back to the boil. Immediately remove pan from heat, cover and leave to stand for about 10 minutes.

Serve each guest with a soft-boiled egg and a bundle of the warm asparagus. Place salt, pepper and a pot of butter on the table so that each person can season the egg to taste and stir in a little butter. The asparagus spears are then dipped into this mixture.

THE HOME GARDEN

There is no reason why salads, other simple vegetables, sage, thyme, marjoram, mint, and other seasonings should not be grown in a well cultivated but comparatively small garden, to be cut fresh for home use when required; and particularly there should always be, if possible, a number of MEDICINAL HERBS grown in the garden. If every father and mother of a family got a herbal guide and studied it in connection with their well selected herbs in the garden, it would give them the treble pleasure of growing their own medicine, doctoring their temporarily sick ones, and thereby keeping them healthier and happier. Therefore, friendly reader, I would say, — If there is not a garden at your home, try and make one, and yourself, your family, and your friends, will be all the happier for it.

The Happifying Gardening Hobby, 1918

ABOUT POTATOES

Reader, if you are at all subject to dyspepsia, beware, oh! beware of waxy or watery potatoes. Mealy potatoes are those that are nutritious, as they contain the greatest amount of gluten, which is the important consideration. The Quarterly states that a club committee were specially called together to select a cook. There were two candidates, an Englishman, from the Albion, and a Frenchman, recommended by Ude; an eminent divine was deputed to examine them, and the first question he put to each was, 'Can you boil a potato?'

The English and Australian Cookery Book, 1864

ON VEGETABLES
The cooking of vegetables being comparatively easy, and also regarded by the amateur as distinctly uninteresting, suffer very considerably at her hands from want of care and attention. As an article of food they are very valuable, the salts they contain purifying the blood, and if taken in sufficient quantity they keep the same in a healthy condition. Unfortunately some of these salts are lost during the process of cooking, and when practicable the water they are boiled in should be reserved for the purpose of making stock.
Australian Economic Cookery Book, 1900

Broad Beans with Bacon

500 g fresh or frozen broad
  beans
1 tablespoon butter
1 clove garlic, crushed
1 onion, finely chopped
2 rashers bacon, chopped

1/2 cup cream
1 tablespoon lemon juice
salt and pepper
1 tablespoon chopped parsley
1 teaspoon chopped winter
  savory or tarragon

Cook the broad beans in salted water until tender, then drain. Melt the butter in a pan and add the garlic, onion and bacon. Sauté until onion is tender, then add the beans. Stir in cream, lemon juice, salt and pepper, and savory or tarragon. Reheat, and add the parsley just before serving.

Cabbage with Lemon and Bacon

1/2 white cabbage
4 rashers bacon, cut into
  strips
1 tablespoon butter
1/2 onion, chopped

1 clove garlic, chopped
juice of 1–2 lemons, to taste
2 tablespoons finely chopped
  parsley
salt and pepper

Slice cabbage fairly thinly, wash and shake dry, then steam in its own liquid until just tender. Put bacon into a saucepan over heat until the fat begins to run, then add the butter, onion and garlic, and sauté until lightly coloured. Add drained cabbage, lemon juice, salt, pepper and parsley. Cover pan and simmer over a medium heat, shaking the pan from time to time until well combined. Serve immediately.

'Brazed' Red Cabbage

½ red cabbage
1 tablespoon butter
1 onion, very finely chopped
2 large apples, diced

3 tablespoons red wine (or use
 cider vinegar)
1 tablespoon sugar
salt and pepper

Shred cabbage and steam in a very little water for a minute or two. Drain well. Into a saucepan put the butter and onion, and sauté until soft. Add apple and cook for a few more minutes, then add the cabbage, wine or vinegar, sugar, salt and pepper. Cover and simmer until tender (about 30 minutes). Add a little water if the juices dry out.

Carrot Puff

3 cups sliced carrots
3 eggs, separated
2 tablespoons chopped chives

pinch of nutmeg
salt and pepper

Steam or boil the carrots for about 10 minutes or until just tender. Drain thoroughly, then place in a blender with the egg yolks, chives, nutmeg, salt and pepper, and purée until smooth. Beat egg whites until stiff and fold into carrot mixture. Spoon into a greased dish set in a baking tin of hot water, and bake in a moderate oven for 30–40 minutes or until puffed and golden.

A piece of bread, the size of an egg, put into the cabbage pot (in muslin) will absorb the bitter juices, and also the smell, while cooking.
The Hobart Cookery Book, 1900

Savoury Cauliflower

1 cauliflower
1 cup cream
1 cup grated cheese

1 wineglass chilli vinegar
a little brandy
salt and cayenne to taste

Steam or boil the cauliflower until just tender. Mash or purée it, then add the cream and cheese followed by the other ingredients. Put into a greased pie dish and bake in a moderate oven until golden (20–30 minutes). Serve very hot.

Brussels Sprouts and Chestnuts

500 g Brussels sprouts
1 tablespoon butter
black pepper
pinch of nutmeg
250 g fresh or canned
  chestnuts

extra 2 tablespoons butter
1 tablespoon sugar
3 tablespoons light beef or
  bacon stock
1 tablespoon red wine
1 tablespoon lemon juice

If using fresh chestnuts, slash each on its flat side and then boil in salted water for 10 minutes. Drain, and remove the skins.

Trim the sprouts, then put them into a pan of boiling salted water and cook until just tender (about 8 minutes). Drain well and return to pan with the butter, pepper and nutmeg, and toss for a few minutes. Serve in the centre of a dish, surrounded by the chestnuts, finished as follows: in a small pan, brown the extra butter with the sugar. Add stock, wine and lemon juice, and boil hard to reduce, then put in the chestnuts and toss to glaze.

Celery Salad

3 heads of celery

1 shallot, cut in half

2 hard-boiled eggs

3 tablespoons oil

$1/2$ teaspoon dry mustard

1 tablespoon vinegar

$1/2$ cup cream

salt and pepper

2–3 anchovies

Slice the celery stalks finely. Rub the salad bowl with the cut shallot. Mix the hard-boiled egg yolks with the oil very gradually, almost drop by drop, and then add the mustard, salt and pepper, anchovies and, finally, the vinegar. Combine the cream with this sauce and spoon over the celery. Garnish with the chopped egg whites.

Jugged Celery

1 kg apples, peeled and
    quartered

1 tablespoon brown sugar

2 rashers bacon (1 kept
    whole, the other finely
    chopped)

2 heads of celery, trimmed

1 onion, finely chopped

3 cloves

1 teaspoon chopped fresh
    rosemary

salt and pepper

Stew the apples with the sugar and 1 tablespoon of water for 20 minutes or until soft. Put the whole bacon rasher in the bottom of an earthenware jug or deep dish and pour in the apple. Stand the sticks of celery upright in the jug, so that the apple comes almost to the top. Sprinkle in the onion, cloves, rosemary, salt, pepper and chopped bacon. Stand the jug in a saucepan of boiling water to come halfway up the sides, cover, and simmer for 2 hours, adding more water as needed. Serve in a bowl.

TO BAKE ONIONS

Choose some large onions, bake them in the oven in their skins, turning occasionally so that they are thoroughly cooked through. Before serving, remove the outer skin, split them open, add a piece of butter, pepper, salt and a little vinegar to each.

CROUTE PARISIENNE AUX CHAMPIGNONS

Take 5 oz of sifted flour, 1 liqueurglassful of water, a little salt, a yolk of egg, and 3 oz of butter. Mix it into a paste, and let it bake 20 minutes in a buttered custard pan in the oven. Peel, wash, and cut up ½ lb of mushrooms and cook them for 5 minutes in water, with a dash of salt and vinegar in it. Chop up 1 onion and put it with 2 oz of butter in a little saucepan on the fire; at the end of 8 minutes sprinkle it with 1 teaspoonful of lemon juice, a liqueurglass of cognac, salt and pepper; let it cook briskly for some minutes over a good fire; add lastly 1 oz of butter, a sprig of chopped parsley, and remove from the fire. Take out the 'croute' or pastry from the oven, and sprinkle the mushrooms on it, serving it hot.

Chokos Stuffed with Seafood

3 chokos (each weighing about 350 g)
1 tablespoon butter
½ cup soft breadcrumbs
4 tablespoons chunky tomato sauce
250 g peeled shrimps or seafood mix
1 tablespoon grated tasty cheese
1 teaspoon chopped fresh thyme
salt and pepper
extra breadcrumbs and butter for baking

Boil the chokos (whole and unpeeled) in salted water until tender (about 30 minutes). Halve, then scoop out the insides to leave a thickish shell. Mash the flesh and cook in a pan with the butter until most of the moisture has evaporated. Mix with the breadcrumbs, tomato sauce, shrimps or seafood mix, tasty cheese and thyme, and season with salt and pepper. Fill the choko halves with this mixture, top with extra breadcrumbs and dot with butter. Bake in a hot oven for 15–20 minutes or until hot and top is crusted brown.

Mushrooms à la Créole

4 tablespoons oil or melted butter
1 cup dry breadcrumbs
1 teaspoon finely chopped garlic
2 tablespoons chopped parsley
1 tablespoon chopped fresh thyme and oregano
500 g largish button mushrooms, stems removed
extra oil
salt and pepper

Put the oil or butter in a baking dish and sprinkle with half of the breadcrumbs, garlic and herbs. Lay on this the mushrooms, then sprinkle with extra oil and cover with the remaining breadcrumbs and herbs. Bake in a hot oven for 20 minutes.

A HORROR OF WASTE

The Goulburn Cookery Book *was compiled by Mrs William Forster Rutledge, of Bungendore. Mrs Rutledge was the daughter of Major Richard Morphy, an Irishman who settled in Australia after serving in India. Her mother was Miss Jane Styles, of Reevesdale, Bungonia. Mr W. F. Rutledge's parents were both Irish.*

Mr and Mrs Rutledge had a horror of waste of any kind. Australia has not always been a land of plenty for the majority, and Ireland never has been. Mrs Rutledge later became almost fanatical on the subject of over-refined foods and, before her death in 1932, wrote a supplement called 'Health Food' which was added to the 1930 and subsequent editions of her book.

The peeling of potatoes was anathema to the Rutledges. Besides the waste of cutting away a sizable amount of potato, the most nutriment in a vegetable is under the skin. Her son nearly caused a mutiny in World War II by trying to dispense with the chore of peeling potatoes in his regiment. The end result was that the men continued to peel away half the potato but did not complain about the chore any more.

The Goulburn Cookery Book, 1973 ed.

POTATO RIBBONS

Wash *2 or 3 potatoes thoroughly. Peel as thinly as possible; then go on peeling them round and round in ribbons in long strips, 1 inch in width. Put them into a cloth, and dry thoroughly. Have a quantity of fat in a stewpan, or saucepan; put the ribbons into a frying-basket, and fry a golden brown. Put on paper to drain, sprinkle with salt, and serve very hot. They are very nice with grilled chops or steaks.*

BAKED PAWPAW
The pawpaw can be used as a vegetable as well as a fruit. Get a pawpaw that is just turning ripe, cut it into quarters, then cut each quarter again, but do not peel it; put it into a baking tin, sprinkle well with salt and pepper; put some dripping in the tin; bake in a very hot oven for twenty minutes.

Parsnip and Macadamia Fritters

1 kg parsnips
2 eggs
1/3 cup melted butter
1 tablespoon flour
1/2 cup milk
1 cup chopped macadamia
  nuts

Steam or boil the parsnips until tender. Blend or purée with the eggs, butter, flour and milk, then stir in the nuts. Deep-fry in spoonfuls until golden-brown, remove with a slotted spoon and drain well before serving.

A Dish of Potatoes

4 large potatoes
2 tablespoons butter
1 clove garlic, chopped
1 cup cream or milk
1/2 cup grated tasty cheese
  (optional)

Slice potatoes into very thin rounds, wash and dry thoroughly in a tea-towel. Butter a gratin dish, then layer in half the potatoes. Dot with half the butter, garlic and cheese (if used). Repeat these layers, then pour the milk or cream gently down the sides of the dish. Cook in a moderate oven for about 1 hour, or at a higher temperature for about 30 minutes.

Halloween Potatoes: 'Champ'

750 g potatoes
6 spring onions, chopped (or
  1 cup peas or chopped
  cabbage)
1 cup milk
salt and pepper

Scrub and boil the potatoes until tender. Meanwhile simmer the spring onions (including the green parts) or peas or cabbage in the milk. Mash the potatoes, then stir in the other vegetables with the milk until the whole is firm but still creamy. Season with salt and pepper, and serve in individual bowls with butter.

To cook a potato and boil an egg are supposed to be two of the simplest of all cooking processes, and yet how few can achieve the desired result.

The Kingswood Cookery Book, n.d.

The potatoe is so essential and desirable an article of food, that too much care cannot be bestowed in their culture and preservation; for should other crops fall short, this will afford the grower a certain means of supporting his family.

W. C. Wentworth, 1820

Soufflé Potatoes

4 good-sized potatoes   *3 egg whites, stiffly beaten*
2 tablespoons butter   *salt*
1/4 cup milk

Wash and scrub the potatoes well, dry them and then bake in a moderate–hot oven for 1–1¼ hours. When cooked, remove and cut each in half with a sharp knife. With a small spoon scoop out the insides, taking care not to damage the skins. Mash the flesh, add the milk and butter, and mix well. Lightly fold in the beaten egg whites and season with salt. Stand the potato halves, cut side up, on a baking-dish and put some of the flesh mixture carefully into each, filling them about half-full. Bake in a hot oven for about 15 minutes, or until pale brown. 'Serve at once on a folded napkin.'

Pumpkin Patties

2 cups mashed pumpkin   *1/2 cup milk*
salt and pepper   *1 teaspoon sugar*
1 dessertspoon tomato ketchup   *pinch of nutmeg*
3 tablespoons melted butter   *butter or bacon fat for frying*

Mix the pumpkin with the salt and pepper, ketchup, butter, milk, nutmeg and sugar. Shape into flat cakes and fry in butter or bacon fat until golden-brown on both sides. Serve hot.

Sugared Sweet Potatoes

750 g sweet potatoes
4 tablespoons butter

4 tablespoons sugar
juice of 1 orange

Wash and cook the sweet potatoes in their skins. Peel, then cut into slices 1-cm thick and put in a single layer in a greased oven dish. Dot with butter and sprinkle with sugar. Place in a moderate oven and bake for about 45 minutes until glazed and brown (sprinkle with the orange juice after about 20 minutes).

Crusted Tomatoes

1 cup breadcrumbs
sugar, salt and pepper to taste
1 1/2 teaspoons finely chopped
 fresh thyme or oregano

4 medium tomatoes
1 egg, beaten
3 tablespoons butter

Combine the breadcrumbs with the sugar, salt, pepper and thyme or oregano. Cut the tomatoes in thick slices. Dip in beaten egg and then coat in the breadcrumb mixture. Fry gently in butter until golden. 'Serve as a vegetable with anything preferred, but they are particularly good with French cutlets or bacon.'

STEWED TOMATOES

Take nice, fresh tomatoes, peel, and slice into a saucepan, and cook slowly for half an hour. Then add salt, a little butter or sweet cream, and a half cup of bread or biscuit crumbs. Sugar may be added if desired.

*A*T THE TABLE

Sauces and Accompaniments

EARLIER GENERATIONS liked to see their tables covered with an array of cruets and gravy boats, which they felt demonstrated both the family's prosperity and the house-wife's skill in entertaining.

In both town and country, sauces and pickles were immensely popular: every table had its condiment container, usually a silver-plated stand with a railing round it that held the various bottles in their correct places, and a tall central handle so that it could be passed easily from one diner to the next. Then there were the jars of pickles, most of them home-made, pickled onions being a particular favourite. In addition there were the hot or cold sauces that the housewife made, usually at the last moment, to accompany each special dish to the table. Even the salt for a dinner was specially mixed, and older books gave the instructions for it: around 100 g of cinnamon, nutmeg, ginger, mace, pimento, cayenne and paprika was added to each 500 g of table salt. In one of her cookery books the Countess of Dudley described no less than forty-four different sauces that should accompany dishes to the table.

Not only the food but the table setting needed hours of work to perfect. First the tablecloth, perhaps of starched damask or of lace, was spread over a pastel cloth beneath. There were elaborate bowls of flowers, sometimes surrounded by fronds of maidenhair (carefully ironed flat), and then there was a sparkling array of polished silver and a variety of wine glasses, one usually holding the starched table-napkin folded in the shape of a bird, a hat or a sunflower.

Today we tend to enjoy our food with the minimum of 'dressing up', but there are occasions when the appetising aroma of a new garnish or sauce, or some elegant frippery at the table, can restore jaded appetites.

OYSTER SAUCE

Heat a dozen oysters in their own liquor in a small saucepan (be careful they do not harden—they should only get plump). Add to a good white sauce, cover, and let stand for 5 minutes.

MOCK CAPERS

Pick young nasturtium seeds when they can be pierced with a needle. Pour over them boiling salted water. Stand 10 minutes covered. Drain at once. Place seed in hot bottle. Pour enough white vinegar in a saucepan, add salt to taste, 1 tablespoon peppercorns, heat to boiling point. Strain over seeds in bottle, cork tightly and stand 10 to 12 days before using. Use in Sauce as Capers to serve with boiled meats and fish.
The Schauer Australian Cookery Book, 1946

White Sauce

2 tablespoons butter
2 tablespoons flour
2½ cups milk (or use half
  milk and half light stock)

1 bay leaf
pinch of nutmeg
salt and pepper to taste

Melt butter in a saucepan over a gentle heat and then stir in the flour, without browning. Remove from heat and gradually add a little of the milk, stirring to remove any lumps. Return to heat and add remainder of milk, still stirring constantly, until well mixed. Add bay leaf, nutmeg, salt and pepper and leave over a gentle heat for 10–20 minutes or until smooth and creamy. Makes about 1½ cups.

VARIATIONS

Parsley Sauce: add 3 tablespoons of chopped parsley at the end of the cooking time.

Caper Sauce: add 2 tablespoons of capers, 1 tablespoon of chopped parsley and a squeeze of lemon juice.

Onion Sauce: add 1 cup of boiled and chopped onions (about 3 medium onions).

Mustard Sauce: add prepared mustard to taste: from 1 teaspoon to 1 tablespoon.

Egg Sauce: add 2 hard-boiled eggs, finely chopped.

Velouté: substitute stock for the milk, and stir in 2 tablespoons of cream at the end of the cooking time.

Lobster or Prawn Sauce for Boiled Fish: add ½ cup of finely chopped lobster or prawns and season with a dash of anchovy sauce and lemon juice to taste.

Brown or Espagnole Sauce

1 rasher bacon, chopped

2 tablespoons butter

$^{1}/_{2}$ onion, finely chopped

1 small carrot, finely chopped

6 button mushrooms, finely
 chopped (optional)

2 tablespoons flour

2$^{1}/_{2}$ cups beef or veal stock

1 bouquet herbs

2 tomatoes, peeled and pulped

2 tablespoons sherry

salt and pepper

Melt the bacon in a pan with the butter. Add the onion, carrot and mushrooms, fry until lightly browned and then stir in the flour. Add the stock, tomatoes, sherry and seasonings, bring slowly to boil and simmer for 20 minutes. Strain before serving with red meat, poultry or game.

VARIATIONS

Madeira Sauce: substitute marsala for the sherry. Serve with ham or liver.

Piquant Sauce for Cutlets, etc.: add 1 tablespoon each of chopped gherkin, chopped capers, chopped shallot, and vinegar, and simmer for 5 minutes.

Bordelaise Sauce for Steak: boil $^{1}/_{4}$ cup chopped shallots with 1 cup red wine until reduced by about half and a moist purée. Add to the brown sauce, simmer for 10 minutes and then whisk in 1 tablespoon of butter and serve.

Apple Sauce for Roast Pork or Goose

4 apples, peeled and sliced

grated rind of $^{1}/_{2}$ lemon

1 tablespoon butter

1 tablespoon water

1 tablespoon sugar

pinch of salt

2 cloves

Put everything into a pan and stew until apples are soft. Remove cloves and beat sauce smooth with a fork.

Remember when you have a tolerable sized party, you must have 2 boats of Fish Sauce, for you have no idea how soon it is ladled away, especially if an inconsiderate young man serves it — he gives half a boat full to the first plate, a Qr. to the next, & will not make it serve 5 persons — if your party is very large, it will be necessary to have a third boat of sauce ready to come up.
Advice to a Young Lady in the Colonies, 1979

BOTTLED SAUCES
Never keep bottles of sauces in the kitchen cupboard. With the exception of one or two special dishes, they should never be used in the kitchen, but always added at table. They are often put into soups and gravies, to mask bad cooking.
The Kingswood Cookery Book, n.d.

SAUCES

Sauces are, as a rule, the stumbling-block of the average cook. Very often the ordinary white sauce is lumpy, pasty, and tasteless, and either too thick or too thin. To make it, do not put a spoonful of flour into a basin, mix with water, and then turn it into boiling milk, adding a lump of butter, and stirring it round two or three times. This is how not to make it. The result is a sort of nasty pudding, very uninviting. The right way is to melt the butter in a small saucepan, add the flour, and cook for a few minutes; then mix in very gradually the cold liquid, either stock, milk, or water, stirring all the time till it boils. It should be put through a straining-cloth or rubbed through a fine hair sieve, and re-heated. This method takes about a quarter of an hour, and a general servant has not often time for it.

The Goulburn Cookery Book, 1899

BIGARADE SAUCE FOR ROAST DUCK

Peel the rind of 2 oranges as thinly as possible, then cut into thin shreds and boil in water for a few minutes. Strain and set aside. Melt 1 tablespoon of butter in a saucepan and then gradually stir in a tablespoon of flour and let it begin to colour a little. Add $^1/_2$ cup stock, salt, pepper and sugar, then the orange rind, and stir until the sauce boils. Add the juice from the oranges and serve.

Imperial Sauce for Squab

2 tablespoons butter
2 tablespoons flour
1¼ cups game or beef stock
½ cup claret

¼ cup sherry
1 dessertspoon redcurrant
 jelly

Melt the butter, stir in the flour, then gradually add the stock. Simmer for 3 minutes, then add wines and redcurrant jelly.

Bread Sauce

1 cup milk
1 small onion, stuck with
 3 cloves
1 blade mace
1 cup fresh breadcrumbs

1 tablespoon butter
2 tablespoons cream
salt, pepper and cayenne to
 taste

Bring the milk to the boil with the onion and mace, then set aside for 15 minutes. Strain, put the milk back into saucepan and add breadcrumbs. Simmer very gently for about 5 minutes, or until sauce begins to thicken, then add the butter, cream and seasonings.

Brown Butter for Brains

4 tablespoons butter
2 tablespoons chopped parsley

1 tablespoon vinegar

Fry the butter in a pan until sizzling and golden (but take care not to burn). Add the parsley and pour butter into dish or sauceboat. Return pan to stove, pour in the vinegar and bring quickly to the boil, then pour over the butter at once.

'ETCETERAS'

To the lovers of gastronomy, hot plates are a positive necessary to a dinner. A local story, well authenticated, is told of an epicure, dining at an hotel in Tasmania. The *garçon* handed a plate so hot that the fingers of the recipient were burnt. With great coolness the *gourmet* put his hand, still smarting from the effects of the caloric, into his pocket and handed the boy a crown, saying, 'Such an unusual circumstance deserved a recompense'. An ill-bred booby, placed in this dilemma, would not have appreciated the luxury, but would have 'uttered curses, not loud but deep'.

The English and Australian Cookery Book, 1864

AN INVITATION TO
DINNER
A premier of Tasmania once
obtained far more political
support from his *dinners* than
the *measures* of his government.
On one occasion, a Member of
the Assembly was returned, and,
as a matter of course, was
expected to join the
Opposition, to which he
belonged. Mr —— invited him
to a *recherché* refection. He
voted with his Amphitryon ever
afterwards, on the
gastronomical rule—that you
ought never to oppose a man
after you have put your legs
under his well-spread
mahogany, at least for a given
number of days, leaving it open
to renew the obligation by a
refresher.
*The English and Australian
Cookery Book*, 1864

Cumberland Sauce for Cold Meats

juice and rind of 1 orange
 and 1 lemon
4 tablespoons redcurrant jelly
1 teaspoon French mustard

salt and pepper
pinch of cayenne or ginger
 (optional)
6 tablespoons port

Peel the rind from the orange and lemon very thinly
and then cut into matchstick strips. Put in a small pan
with 1 cup of water, bring to the boil and then strain.
Gently melt the redcurrant jelly in a small pan, then
add the mustard, salt and pepper, and cayenne or
ginger if used. Stir until mustard dissolves, add port and
fruit juices, then cook for a further 5 minutes. Stir in the
orange and lemon peel, and chill before serving.

Piquant Salad Cream

2 eggs
½ cup sugar
1 cup white vinegar
a nut of butter

1 cup milk
1 teaspoon dry mustard
good pinch of salt

Break the eggs into a bowl, add the sugar and vinegar
(vinegar left in the jar from pickled gherkins, etc. can be
used up, and adds flavour), and beat until coloured and
frothy. Melt the butter in a pan, pour in the egg mixture
and set aside. Put a little of the milk into a bowl, stir in
the mustard and salt, then the rest of the milk, and add
this mixture to the saucepan. Place over a low heat and
stir constantly until the mixture becomes creamy like
honey (do not let it boil), which only takes a few
minutes.

 'If placed in a screw-top jar in a Coolgardie safe, this
will keep for 3 weeks.'

ETIQUETTE OF DINNER PARTIES

DINNER PARTIES. *A dinner party should consist of an equal number of gentlemen and ladies, those being invited who it is thought will like to meet. If there are no young people belonging to the house, it is very common not to invite the daughters of the married couples; but if any young lady is invited, care should be taken that a suitable escort is provided for her. It is not necessary to introduce all the members of the party to each other: in a friend's house all talk to each other without introduction, and without this forming any subsequent acquaintance, unless such is desired by both parties. It is as well, however, to introduce the two first comers, as it avoids the preliminary stiffness. The due precedence of the party has, of course, been duly studied by the hostess before her guests arrive, and she has also arranged which gentleman should take each lady. It is the duty of the host to introduce the gentlemen to the ladies whom they are to escort, but very frequently the hostess performs this duty for him.*

MENU CARDS. Now that dîners à la Russe are universal menu cards are indispensable. There should be one to every couple. Dinners are neither so long nor so heavy as was formerly the case. Two soups, handed round together, two kinds of fish, also handed together, whitebait, when in season, two entrées handed in succession, boiled fowl and roast lamb or mutton handed together, quails and ducklings (or any other two second-course dishes) handed together, a hot and a cold sweet dish in succession, and some preparation of cheese, such as ÉCLAIRS RAMEQUINS, or cheese-straws, is an ample menu for any dinner-party, no matter of how many members it may consist. In large parties two dishes of each entrée and of each sweet are prepared, so that the two sides of the table are served simultaneously by two waiters.

The Housewife's Treasury of Domestic Information, n.d.

SERVICE FRANCAIS

Sur chaque couvert, placer la serviette pliée avec le morceau de pain dessous; le menu, sur lequel est inscrit le nom de l'invité, à côté des verres qui sont devant l'assiette.

Il faut autant de verres qu'il y a de services, verres à Madère, ordinaire, à Bordeaux, coupe, verre à Oporto et à liqueurs. Les pièces sont d'abord apportées entières, et emportées pour le découpage, puis reviennent, toutes decoupées, pour le service.

Le déjeuner de midi commence par les hors-d'oeuvre. A diner, ce service est généralement remplacé par le potage. Les légumes, à moins qu'ils n'aient été cuits en entrée avec la viande se servent séparément, après le rôti.

The Australian Household Guide, 1916

TO CLEAR THE CLOTH

A bungler at this is a source of much confusion at the dinner table. The waitress should be soft-footed, neat, and silent of tongue, with observant eyes, and ready, willing hands. There must be two trays for the knives and forks, were they collected in one the latter would get scratched. The carving knife and fork should be removed first, then the joint and vegetables, and lastly the plates. These can be gathered together by simply removing each knife and fork and placing the plates beneath each other till all are there, separating the knives and forks at the side-board. Collect all the glasses, water-bottles, etc., on a tray as they were brought in, and take them out of the room at once. Pieces of bread should be lifted with a fork into the tray, and, lastly, with a crumb-brush brush away the crumbs on to a small tray. Fold the table-cloth in the creases, press it if you have a press, and place it in the sideboard drawer. The next process is to bring in a neat dust-pan and small brush, and lightly brush up the crumbs from the floor.

The Housewife's Treasury of Domestic Information, n.d.

HOUSEHOLD HINT
To mix mustard, put the
required amount in the pot,
add a pinch of salt, and mix
with vinegar. This will keep
without crusting.
The Green and Gold Cookery Book,
1928

Mango Mayonnaise

¹/₂ cup chopped mango   *1 tablespoon grainy mustard*
¹/₂ cup mayonnaise   *2 tablespoons chopped fresh*
1 tablespoon lemon juice   *basil or mint*

Purée mango in a blender with half the mayonnaise. Stir
in the remaining mayonnaise with the lemon juice,
mustard and herbs. Serve with cold poultry.

VARIATIONS
Apple Mayonnaise: substitute puréed apple for the
mango, use mint rather than basil, and use grated
horseradish instead of the mustard for a sharper
contrast. This is delicious with duck.
Avocado Mayonnaise: substitute avocado for the mango.
Omit the lemon juice, mustard and herbs, and add
instead a tablespoon of tomato sauce and a dash of
Tabasco.

Horseradish Sauce

1 tablespoon grated fresh   *1 teaspoon sugar*
  horseradish (or 1¹/₂   *¹/₄ teaspoon salt*
  teaspoons bottled   *1 teaspoon prepared mustard*
  horseradish)   *3 tablespoons thick cream,*
1 dessertspoon vinegar   *lightly whipped*

Mix everything together, adding the cream last.

Tartare Sauce

1 cup mayonnaise   *1 teaspoon lemon juice*
1 tablespoon chopped parsley   *1 teaspoon (or more) chopped*
1 tablespoon chopped shallots   *capers*
  or spring onions
1 teaspoon chopped gherkins

Mix all the ingredients together and serve cold.

Chestnut Croquettes for Game

1 dessertspoon butter	1 egg, beaten
1 small onion, chopped	1/4 cup flour
1 cup unsweetened chestnut	extra beaten egg for coating
purée	1/2 cup dry breadcrumbs
salt and pepper	oil or butter for frying

Heat the butter in a small pan, add the onion and cook gently until transparent. Add to the chestnut purée and mix well. Add salt and pepper, and bind with the egg. Form into small balls, roll in flour and beaten egg, then breadcrumbs. Fry in oil or butter until golden-brown.

Yorkshire Pudding

1 cup plain flour	1 egg
salt	1 1/4 cups milk

Sift the flour and salt into a bowl, make a well in the centre and add the egg and milk. Mix together, beat well and leave to stand for 1 hour. Brush muffin tins generously with melted butter and preheat in a hot oven for a few minutes. Stir the batter again and then fill each tin two-thirds full. Bake for about 15 minutes or until well risen and golden-brown.

For a savoury version, add 2 teaspoons of chopped fresh herbs and 1 tablespoon of finely chopped onion to the batter.

HORSERADISH
The flavour of horseradish is exceedingly pungent and apt to 'run up the nose'.
Tom Stobart, n.d.

SAUCE A LA RIMOLADE
Put into a sauceboat a shalot, chervil, chives, a head of garlic, all chopped very fine; salt and pepper; beat it up with mustard, oil, and vinegar.

FORCEMEATS AND STUFFINGS

The ability of the cook is always determined by his or her forcemeats and stuffing. We can describe the latter, and can only hint at the ingredients of the former, for they may be said to comprise Legion. Every variety of meat: hams, tongues, crumbs of bread, flour, dripping, and herbs, spices, curry-powder, anchovies, prawns and crabs, eggs and sauces—in truth, forcemeat may be made from any and every thing. The great desideratum is to allow the taste of no one article to overpower the others, or otherwise it is decidedly imperfect in its composition. Stuffing and forcemeat has been always considered as the CHEF D'OEUVRE of the CUISINE, for a bad cook cannot manipulate good forcemeat: such a circumstance would be a culinary paradox.

Forcemeat Balls for Fish, Soups, &c.—Beat the flesh and soft parts of a medium-sized lobster or crayfish, half an anchovy, a large piece of boiled celery, the yolk of an egg, hard-boiled, a little cayenne, mace, salt, and pepper, with two table-spoonfuls of bread crumbs, two ounces of butter, and two eggs, well beaten up; make into balls, and fry of a light brown.

The English and Australian Cookery Book, 1864

THINGS TO BE REMEMBERED

That fried croutons are served with pea soup.

That apple sauce is served with roast goose and roast pork.

That red currant jelly is served with roast saddle of mutton.

That mint sauce is served with roast lamb.

That bread sauce is served with roast turkey and roast fowl.

That egg sauce is served with boiled fish.

That melted butter, or white sauce, is served with boiled fowls.

That caper sauce is served with boiled mutton, and sometimes onion sauce.

That onion sauce is served with boiled rabbit and boiled bandicoot.

That parsley sauce is often served with boiled mutton and boiled fish.

The Antipodean Cookery Book, 1895

Forcemeat Balls for Pies, Poultry, etc.

1 cup fresh breadcrumbs
1 tablespoon suet
salt and pepper
2 tablespoons chopped fresh
  herbs
rind of 1/2 lemon, finely
  chopped
1 small egg, beaten

Mix the crumbs and suet together, and season well. Add
the herbs and lemon rind, and bind with the beaten
egg. Roll mixture into small balls and fry in hot oil or
butter.

Raisin Stuffing for Wild Game

1 1/2 cups fresh breadcrumbs
a little milk
1/4 teaspoon salt
1/4 teaspoon pepper
1/2 cup chopped parsley
1 tablespoon melted butter
1 egg, beaten
1/2 cup chopped raisins
1/4 cup chopped celery

Place the breadcrumbs in a bowl and add the salt,
pepper, parsley and melted butter, then the eggs. Lastly
add the raisins and celery, mixing well.

DEVILLED MUSCATELS

Heat oil in a pan and in it fry
one cupful of muscatels until
golden. Drain, then dust over
with salt, cayenne and ground
ginger, and serve in fancy
paper. Sufficient for four
persons; these should be served
after game.

Desserts and Other Confections

IN THE COOKERY BOOKS of our grandmothers we see page after page of recipes for solid puddings, full of sugar and suet and butter, that were put into a basin and boiled or steamed for several hours. It was usual to serve these puddings at every main meal, both winter and summer, and we can feel real sympathy for the housewives compelled to keep stoking up their stoves to keep the pot on the boil. Hampered as they were, in long skirts and high-necked blouses, with full petticoats underneath, it is not surprising that so many of their cookery books carried advertisements for the new rustless corsets that put an end to the annoyance of hot, clinging blouses ruined by rustmarks. 'Think what this means in warm climates', reminded the advertiser.

Next in popularity to steamed and boiled puddings came pies and tarts, again calling for a 'bright fire'. Baked puddings, custards and hot fritters were other standbys, and when a cold sweet was served it was often with an apology. Even cold desserts were apt to be very solid custards, or trifles made from rich sponge cake. Admittedly jellies were great favourites but there was always the awful question 'Will it set?'. Until the advent of refrigeration, ice-cream remained beyond the bounds of possibility, except in a few sophisticated city households that owned mechanical 'freezers'. It was left for Hannah Maclurcan to pioneer chilled sweets and make them popular. Dr Philip Muskett and Mrs Colcord followed with many innovative dishes using fresh fruit: how delighted they would be to see today's tables, with their abundance of fruit and iced desserts.

AN APPLE PIE

Make a puff paste; lay some round the sides of the dish. Pare and quarter your apples; lay a thick row with half the sugar you intend to use. Mince a little lemon peel fine; add to the apples with a little of the juice and a few cloves here and there; then the rest of your apples and sugar and a little more lemon. Boil the peel and cores of the apples in a little water and a blade of mace till it is very good; strain it, and boil the syrup with a little sugar till there is very little; pour it into your pie, put on the upper crust, and bake for an hour to an hour and a half, according to size. A little quince or marmalade is an improvement.

Apple Amber Pudding

750 g apples, peeled and
   sliced
2 tablespoons butter
1/3 cup sugar

thinly peeled rind of 1 lemon
3 eggs, separated
2 teaspoons castor sugar
pinch of salt

Stew the apples gently with the butter, sugar and lemon rind. Pass through a sieve, stir in 2 of the egg yolks and beat well. When cool, pour into a greased pie dish and bake in a hot oven for 20 minutes. Beat the egg whites, castor sugar and salt until very stiff and then pile on top of the apple. Bake in a cool oven until meringue is pale brown.

'Peaches, halved and sprinkled with sugar then baked until tender, may be finished in the same way. Serve cold.'

Brown Betty

1 kg apples
2 cups fresh breadcrumbs
1/2 cup melted butter
1/2 cup brown sugar

juice and grated rind of 1
   lemon
1 teaspoon ground cinnamon

Peel, core and slice the apples. Mix the breadcrumbs with the butter and place one-third of mixture in a buttered pie dish. Combine apples, sugar, lemon juice and rind, and the cinnamon. Put half of this mixture in the dish, then repeat layers, finishing with crumbs. Bake in a moderate oven for 30 minutes and serve with plenty of cream.

APPLE PUDDINGS AND PIES

These kind of puddings and pies are, after plum puddings, also a national dish. The sort of fruit for cookery, according to all writers on pomology, should be juicy, full of flavour, and apt to pulp when done. The crust for puddings and pies we have given elsewhere, and in using the fruit a little lemon is an improvement to their flavour, or a few quinces cut up.

The editor of 'Hints for the Table' states a fact that we are desirous of giving further publicity to, in the hope that it will receive attention from those of the fair sex now living in 'single blessedness'. It is, that once upon a time 'a clever man chose his wife by making an apple pudding'. Who can doubt his sense and discernment? Love at first sight will become exploded, and love at first taste will now take its place. The drapery misses—that is, ladies furnished, on credit, with articles of attire, to be repaid on marriage—will fall into desuetude, and those young ladies who can work into proper shape an apple pudding will most properly be in request at the temple of Hymen.

The English and Australian Cookery Book, 1864

OF ORCHARD PESTS

The apple has a great enemy in a minute insect called the Cochineal, owing more, perhaps, to its being nearly of the same colour, than from any resemblance to the Spanish insect of that name. A gentleman who had eight trees that had for several years borne a delicious apple, had the mortification to find the whole of his trees at once infested by those insects in excessive number; after which they left off bearing, and after failing in many experiments to relieve them, he came unwillingly to the resolution of cutting down the trees . . . A gardener of the Colony, who has attended a good deal to this matter, affirms that a weed called the Churnwort presents a perfect remedy to the disaster; with this weed, the roots, cleared of the earth, and the branches also, he advises to be thoroughly well rubbed.

W. C. Wentworth, 1820

FIG SALAD

Skin and halve the figs. Put a layer in a glass dish, sprinkle with sugar, add another layer of skinned figs, more sugar, and so on. Cool in ice chest, and just before serving add a liqueur-glass of liqueur.

Quinces Stewed and Baked

1 cup sugar
2½ cups water
4 quinces, peeled and
  quartered

¼ cup orange juice
2 teaspoons grated orange
  rind

Make a syrup of the sugar and water, and bring to the boil. Put in the quinces and simmer for about an hour or until they are tender. Remove with a slotted spoon, put in a pie dish with a few spoonfuls of the syrup, the orange juice and rind, and bake in a slow oven for ½–1 hour, until they are dark red. Serve cold, in a glass dish.

Traditional Syllabub

2 tablespoons brandy
5 tablespoons sherry or white
  wine
rind and juice of 1 lemon

2 tablespoons sugar
1¼ cups thick cream
pinch of nutmeg

Combine brandy, wine or sherry, and lemon rind in a bowl and set aside for a few hours or overnight. Strain into another bowl and then stir in the sugar until dissolved. Add the cream gradually and then beat gently with a whisk until mixture holds its shape. Spoon into individual bowls and chill before serving with macaroons or sponge biscuits.

Croûte de Cerises

3 cups pitted cherries   pinch of salt
3 tablespoons flour   3½ cups milk
3 eggs   3 tablespoons castor sugar

Put flour and salt in a bowl and break in the eggs, one by one. Add milk gradually, and then stir in the sugar. Place the cherries in an ovenproof dish and pour egg mixture over. Bake in a moderate oven for 30 minutes or until set and serve with extra sugar sprinkled on top.

Mousse au Chocolat: 'A French Receipt'

175 g dark cooking chocolate   1 dessertspoon rum or brandy
3 tablespoons water   3 eggs, separated
1 tablespoon butter   cream for serving

Break the chocolate into pieces and melt gently in a small pan with the water, stirring constantly. Remove from heat and add the butter and the rum or brandy. While the mixture is still hot, stir in the egg yolks. Beat the egg whites until stiff and fold into the chocolate mixture. Spoon into one large or four small dishes and refrigerate overnight. Serve with whipped cream.

Apricot Mousse

500 g apricots   ½ cup cream
¼–½ cup sugar, to taste   2 egg whites, stiffly beaten
a little water

Stew the apricots in very little water until soft. Sieve or purée in a blender and add sugar to taste. Allow to cool and then stir in the whipped cream. Lastly, fold in the egg whites. Refrigerate before serving.

SPRAY FOR FRUIT TREES
Little's sheep dip, 1 in 100;
¾ lb starch to 100 gallons.
Spray twice in November and December, and once in January.

TO REMOVE THE STAINS OF FRUIT FROM THE HANDS
Wash your hands in clear water, dry slightly, and while yet moist, strike a sulphur match and hold your hands around the flame. The stains will immediately disappear.
Australian Economic Cookery Book, 1900

ITALIAN CREAM

An elegant dish. Boil a pint and a half of milk, and when it is boiling infuse the peel of an orange and a lemon until the milk is flavoured. Put in a little salt, three ounces of pounded lump sugar, and the yolks of six eggs; add a sufficient quantity of isinglass, dissolved, to make it tenacious; put it into moulds until cold. To take it from the mould, dip a cloth in hot water, and rub round the mould; the cream will then turn out entire.

Passionfruit Cream (la Cornishe)

24 passionfruit
juice of $1/2$–1 lemon, to taste
$2^1/_2$ cups cream
$1/_3$ cup castor sugar
1 tablespoon gelatine

Put the passionfruit pulp in a bowl with the lemon juice. Beat cream and castor sugar until thickish but not stiff. Dissolve gelatine over heat, strain and add to cream. Mix in passionfruit pulp and spoon into passionfruit skins or glass dishes. Refrigerate until set.

Pouding Glacé aux Fruits

$2^1/_2$ cups milk
1 stick vanilla pod
$1/_4$ cup castor sugar
chopped rind of 1 lemon
10 egg yolks
1 teaspoon vanilla essence
$2^1/_2$ cups cream, stiffly
   whipped
1 teaspoon castor sugar
4 tablespoons brandy
$2/_3$ cup maraschino
$1/_2$ cup any kind dried fruit,
   finely chopped

Bring the milk to the boil with vanilla, castor sugar and chopped lemon peel. Cover the pan and leave aside to steep for 10 minutes. Remove the vanilla pod, mix the milk with the egg yolks and vanilla essence, return to pan and stir over gentle heat until the mixture thickens. Strain, leave to cool and then partly freeze mixture. Combine whipped cream with castor sugar, brandy and maraschino, then stir into partly frozen custard mixture. Add dried fruit and re-freeze.

Caramel Custard

¹/₂ cup water
¹/₂ cup sugar
2¹/₂ cups milk
sugar to taste

3 whole eggs plus 1 yolk
¹/₄ teaspoon vanilla essence or
a splash of brandy

To make the caramel, gently heat the water and sugar until dissolved, then turn heat up to medium and boil until a rich golden-brown. Line small moulds with the caramel, turning the moulds so they are coated thoroughly. Leave to set.

Heat the milk very gently with sugar to taste. Beat the eggs and yolk and pour hot milk over, mixing well. Flavour with vanilla or brandy, as preferred. Pour the custard into the lined moulds and place in a baking dish of hot water. Steam gently in a slow–moderate oven for about 45 minutes or until set.

Devonshire Junket

2¹/₂ cups milk
1 dessertspoon sugar
2 tablespoons brandy or rum

1 teaspoon rennet
whipped cream to serve
cinnamon or nutmeg

Warm the milk just a little and add sugar and brandy or rum. Stir in the rennet and leave to stand in a cool place until set. Serve topped with a dollop of whipped cream and a sprinkling of cinnamon or nutmeg.

'The rum may be omitted, and it is sometimes preferred unsweetened. An excellent dish for children and invalids. It may be served with stewed fruit or jam.'

CURD CHEESECAKES

Take 1¹/₂ pints of new milk, 1 beaten egg, 1 dessertspoonful of rennet, 1 dessertspoonful of brandy, 1 tablespoonful of sugar, currants, and chopped peel. Take the new milk, warm it, and curdle with a dessertspoonful of rennet. Break the curd, and drain the whey from it through muslin. Add to the curd a beaten egg, the brandy, sugar, chopped peel, and currants to taste. Line some patty pans with good puff paste, or, better still, a nice short crust, half fill them with the mixture, and bake till delicately browned.

HOW TO FREEZE WITHOUT
A MACHINE

Break up the ice into small pieces, and put it into the outer vessel in alternate layers with the salt—say, for instance, a bucket; put the mixture into a billy-can or anything that would do as well; cover it well with the ice and salt; keep stirring and shaking it until the mixture is set; if wanted for a cream it will then be ready for use, but if wanted for iced puddings you must turn it into a mould and place it back into the ice, but do not stir it any more; when it is required turn it out on to a glass dish. Of course, where people have ice cream machines it is very simple.

Mrs Maclurcan's Cookery Book,
1898

Cardinal Ice

4 cups ripe raspberries   2¹/₂ cups water
juice of 1 lemon   ¹/₄ cup maraschino
1 cup sugar   ¹/₄ cup red curaçao

Mash the raspberries, add the lemon juice and sugar, then set aside for an hour. Press through a sieve, add water, maraschino and curaçao, then freeze. Serve in glasses.

Roman Ice

1 cup sugar   1 cup lemon juice
3 cups water

Dissolve the sugar with the water in a pan, stirring constantly. Simmer for 5 minutes, then remove from heat and stir in the lemon juice. Leave aside to cool. Strain into a shallow pan and place in the freezer for 30 minutes. Scrape the ice into flakes with a fork, return to freezer for 2 hours and then repeat this process every half hour. Once the mixture is slushy, serve in chilled glasses garnished with borage flowers or mint leaves.

Crème de Pain Bis

3 cups fresh wholemeal   ¹/₂ cup sugar
   breadcrumbs   2 eggs, separated
2 tablespoons brandy or rum
2¹/₂ cups cream

Spread the breadcrumbs on a baking tray and bake in a moderate–hot oven until crisp and lightly browned. Beat the cream with the sugar, then add the brandy or rum and the egg yolks, and beat well again. Fold in the cooked crumbs. Beat the egg whites until stiff, fold into crumb mixture, and freeze.

   'This is a good entremet or dessert ice, and is much liked for garden and evening parties.'

MRS MACLURCAN

Hannah Maclurcan played a leading role in introducing a wide range of desserts early this century, first into good restaurants and then, by medium of her cookery book, into Australian homes.

Hannah Maclurcan's career was as spectacular as the sales of her book. Born Hannah Phillips in the mining town of Tambooroora, close to Hill End in the Bathurst district, she went with her family to Queensland when mining declined. In Queensland the Phillips family had interests in hotels, and at the age of seventeen the capable young Hannah was managing the Club Hotel in Toowoomba for her father. The Club was noted for its big airy rooms opening onto wide verandahs, and for its huge stables, but especially for its excellent cuisine. As the Darling Downs prospered it became the natural meeting place for rich and influential local families.

Hannah was left a widow when still very young. Her second husband was Captain Charles Maclurcan of the RSN Co's Merkera, and with him she moved to Townsville to take over the Queen's Hotel. It was here that Mrs Maclurcan tempted diners (who no doubt were feeling limp and enervated in that hot moist climate) with her original cuisine. In place of the apple, pear or cherry sweets to which they were accustomed, guests were tempted by a wide range of jellies, sorbets and ices made from fruits they barely knew – rosellas, granadillas, passionfruit, mulberries, quinces and guavas. There was even a jelly made from prickly pear, which most people regarded with loathing as a noxious weed but which Mrs Maclurcan described as 'most delicious, having the richest colour of any of our native fruits'.

In the early years of this century the Maclurcans moved to Sydney, where they took over the Wentworth Hotel. It was a luxurious hotel, with eighty superb suites, and here Mrs Maclurcan had her greatest triumphs. When she heard that the Prince of Wales was to visit Australia in 1920, knowing of his love for dancing she immediately added another floor to the Wentworth to provide a ballroom with space for a thousand diners and dancers. No matter how long or how tedious the Prince's official engagements in Sydney might be, as soon as he was free he made his way to the Wentworth to dance till dawn, fortified no doubt by its cocktails and tropical fruit ices.

MRS MACLURCAN'S PRICKLY PEAR JELLY

 The prickly pear is a fruit seldom used, although if properly treated is most delicious; it has the richest colour of any of our native fruits, for jam or jelly it needs no water whatever.

If required for jam you must be most careful to see that all the prickles are removed, otherwise it may be unpleasant to get one of those nasty little things in your mouth; for jelly, of course, it has all to be strained, so should you leave a few in it would not be so serious.

1 lb prickly pears	1 cup sugar
2 lemons	3 ozs gelatine
1 quart water	2 glasses sherry

Get the prickly pears, rub them in sand or sawdust with your boot or a piece of wood until all the prickles are removed, then cut them into four pieces; squeeze the juice of the two lemons in with them, put them into the saucepan with the water and sugar, allow them to boil for two hours; should they require more lemon juice put in the juice of another half, then strain, put back into a saucepan and allow it to boil with the gelatine and sherry until the gelatine is dissolved; strain and put into wet moulds, place on the ice until set.

FROM THE EARL OF KILMOREY

June 18th 1900. *98 Eaton Place, S.W.,*

M*RS* H*ANNAH* M*ACLURCAN* *is personally well known to me. In a place like Queensland, where one hardly expects the perfection of cooking and hotel management, it was my good fortune to come across the Queen's Hotel, at Townsville, when my experience of* M*RS* M*ACLURCAN*, *the then Proprietoress, satisfied me that she could not only superintend cooking, but could talk and write about it to perfection.*

To many of my friends I have recommended her Australian book, and I am pleased to learn that M*RS* M*ACLURCAN* *is publishing an English Version.*

Faithfully yours,

(Signed) K*ILMOREY*.

DESSERT

It is a common practice with many parents to give their children permission to ask for and obtain what they like of the dessert from their own table, the children coming down from their nursery for this purpose. This is a cruel kindness. The simple, well-cooked, and much enjoyed dinner they may have had is quite marred by this after loading of rich things. But as children should *not* be called upon to *see* food they cannot help coveting, without being allowed to eat of it, some other time should be chosen for their appearance downstairs than the dessert hour, or else strict supervision as to what they do eat should be exercised.

The Housewife's Treasury of Domestic Information, n.d.

Christmas Pudding

4 cups fresh breadcrumbs
1 cup flour
1 cup melted butter
1¹/₂ cups raisins
1¹/₂ cups sultanas
1¹/₂ cups currants
2 cups soft brown sugar
³/₄ cup candied peel, chopped
1 teaspoon ground nutmeg

1 teaspoon mixed spice
rind and juice of 1 lemon and 1 orange
1¹/₄ cups ground almonds (or use grated carrot)
1 teaspoon salt
6 eggs, beaten
¹/₂ cup brandy, rum or beer

In a large bowl mix together all the dry ingredients. Melt the butter and stir into mixture, then add the beaten eggs, brandy, and juices. Put into two well-greased basins and steam or boil for 8 hours.

Queen of Puddings

2¹/₂ cups milk
4 tablespoons butter
2¹/₂ cups fresh breadcrumbs
1 tablespoon sugar
grated rind of 1 lemon

4 eggs, separated
¹/₄ cup castor sugar
2 tablespoons or more berry jam

Bring milk to boil with the butter, then stir into the breadcrumbs with the sugar and lemon rind. Allow to cool a little and then beat in the egg yolks. Pour into a greased pie dish, and bake in a moderate oven for 30 minutes or until just firm. Remove, cool and spread with jam. Beat the egg whites with the castor sugar until stiff. Pile onto the cooked base, sprinkle with a little extra sugar and bake until lightly browned (about 15 minutes). Serve with cream.

Broken Hill Pudding

2 cups flour
1 cup sugar
1 cup each of currants, dates
  and raisins or figs
1 tablespoon butter, dissolved
  in ³/₄ cup boiling water

1 dessertspoon bicarbonate of
  soda, dissolved in 1 cup
  boiling water
juice and rind of ¹/₂ lemon

Mix all the ingredients together, put in a greased basin and steam in a pot of boiling water for 2¹/₂ hours.

Hard Sauce for Plum Puddings, etc.

1 cup butter
¹/₃ cup icing sugar
3 tablespoons brandy or rum

generous pinch of ground
  nutmeg

Beat the butter and sugar together until mixture looks like whipped cream. Add the brandy gradually until well mixed, and finally mix in the nutmeg. Pile up in a glass bowl.

'It is also very good with hot apple pudding or any fruit pudding.'

Foam Sauce

1 cup sugar
2 eggs, separated
1 tablespoon brandy, sherry or
  wine

a nut of butter

Beat the sugar and egg yolks together. Stand the basin in a saucepan of boiling water, add the butter, and stir until quite hot. Add the stiffly beaten whites, and stir in the brandy just before serving.

FRUIT CREAM FOR COLD PUDDINGS
Half a cup of passionfruit, which has been put through a fine sieve to free it from seeds, added to half a cup of raw cream, a teaspoonful of brandy, and sugar to taste. Apricot or other jam (heated and passed through sieve) can be used instead of passionfruit, but then the brandy must be omitted.

PEACH MARRIAGE

A RECIPE SPECIALLY FOR CHEFS

In preparing this delightful dish the greatest care must be taken in the selection of the fruit. This should not be done in haste, and due consideration should be given to the tree from which the peach is gathered. Some peaches have a golden hue, but this should not influence the choice. What is essential is not the outside appearance, but to be sure the peach is sound. Unless it is good to the heart the dish will be a failure.

In some cases an artificial bloom is added, but it is questionable if this is an improvement. It certainly does not enhance the flavor, and unless handled with care is likely to leave marks on the 'chef's' clothes.

Having selected the peach, take it to the receptacle, which should be neat if not ornate. Do not skin it. If it has a golden hue let it remain the property of the fruit. Handle it tenderly, giving frequent applications of sugar, for sweetness is the most delicious part of the dish.

Occasionally it may ferment. Should it do so do not lose your temper or express yourself with cross words. This has never been found to do any good. Rather, if a smoker, calm yourself by communing with 'Lady Nicotine', or, better still, go into the garden and try and absorb the love spirit of the Giver of Flowers. After an interval inspect the peach again, and if fermentation has ceased, add a little sugar. Should it still continue, a little spice may be added, but this should be done judiciously.

With care the dish may be kept for a long time. It will eventually attain a silver hue, and later a golden tinge.

The Green and Gold Cookery Book, 1928

Chocolate Ping-pong Balls

4 cups chopped dates *1 cup melted chocolate*
1 cup crunchy peanut butter

Mash the dates to a paste. With floured hands shape
spoonfuls of the peanut butter into balls, then press
around each a layer of the date paste. Roll them around
between your hands, then dip one at a time in the
melted chocolate. Set aside in a cool place to harden.

Simple Caramels

1 cup cream *1 teaspoon vanilla essence*
2 cups sugar

Combine the cream and sugar and boil, stirring all the
time, for 10 minutes Add the essence, then pour on
buttered plates and cut into squares.

Barley Sugar

1 1/2 cups sugar *1/2 teaspoon cream of tartar*
1/2 cup hot water

Combine ingredients in a pan over a medium heat;
watch carefully, but do not stir. Boil until mixture turns
an amber colour, then turn out onto a buttered dish.

'THE GOOD LITTLE
NORMEY'
Mix equal quantities of Sun-
Raysed sultanas, Sun-Raysed
currants and Sun-Raysed seeded
lexias. Put through a mincer;
roll into little balls, and coat
with desiccated coconut.

Cakes, Breads and Sandwiches

TEA ON THE LAWN, that transcendently English institution, was at the height of fashion in the late eighteenth century and persisted among the middle and upper classes for many decades to come. As late as the 1930s such cookbooks as that by Lady Sysonby in London would elaborate at some length on the requirements of the tea table:

> A tea table without a big cake in the country in England would look very bare and penurious. The ideal tea table should include some sort of hot buttered toast or scone, one or two sorts of sandwiches, a plate of small light cakes, and our friend the luncheon cake.
>
> Add a pot of jam or honey, and a plate of brown and white bread and butter – which I implore my readers not to cut too thin – and every eye will sparkle . . .

The ceremony was, naturally, adopted in the colonies. Cakes played the main role in the development of teas as 'occasions': hostesses were immensely proud of the lightness of their sponges and of the enormous number of different cakes that they could produce. Lady Hackett's cookery book gave recipes for no less than 232 different cakes and typical of the tea parties of that era was her suggested menu for 'An Engaged Girl's Tea': the recipes included innumerable dainties with the fanciful names of Bachelor's Buttons, Variety Cake, Fairy Cake, Lady's Fingers, Ring Cake, Sweetheart Biscuits, Passion Fruit Cake and Love in Ambush.

Of course, scones, biscuits and breads have always been part of the tea menu, too. The recipes that follow offer a selection of the most enduring tea-time delights, including crunchy Anzacs, which were baked by the hundred in kitchens all over Australia during the First World War and posted away to the Front.

LEMON SPONGE

Take four eggs, one cup of sugar, one tablespoonful of lemon juice, with a little of the grated rind and one cupful of flour; beat the yolks of the eggs to a foam, then beat in the sugar, adding a little at a time; then add the lemon juice and grated rind; beat the whites of the eggs until very stiff, then lightly fold and chop them into the mixture. Slowly sift in the flour, carefully working it in. Do not beat after the flour has been added. Bake in two layers and put together with fruit jelly or lemon honey.

Simplest Sponge Cake

³/₄ cup castor sugar

3 eggs

¹/₄ cup butter

2 tablespoons water

1 cup self-raising flour

PASSIONFRUIT FILLING

6 passionfruit

1 dessertspoon arrowroot

¹/₄ cup water

4 tablespoons butter

¹/₂ cup sugar

2 eggs, separated

Beat the castor sugar with the eggs until foamy. Melt the butter very gently with the water, allow to cool a little and then stir into the egg mixture. Last, fold in the flour. Pour into two greased and floured sandwich tins and bake in a moderate oven for 20 minutes. Sandwich together with Passionfruit Filling (or with jam, or fresh berries when available) and whipped cream.

To make the filling, remove the pulp from the passionfruit and strain away half the seeds. Mix the arrowroot with a little of the water and bring the rest to the boil with the butter and sugar. Stir in the arrowroot, remove pan from heat, add the egg yolks and then the juice, then return pan to stove. Stir carefully, without boiling, until mixture thickens. Allow to cool before using to sandwich the cakes together.

Rich Dark Ginger Cake

1/2 cup butter
3/4 cup soft brown sugar
2 eggs
2 cups plain flour
1 cup treacle
1/2 cup sliced preserved ginger

1/3 cup sultanas or raisins
1 teaspoon ground ginger
1/2 teaspoon bicarbonate of
  soda
2 tablespoons milk

Soften the butter a little and beat with the sugar until creamy. Add the eggs, beating well, and then add, one at a time, the flour, treacle, sultanas, and preserved and ground gingers. Warm the milk, stir in the bicarbonate of soda and add this mixture to the other ingredients. Grease and flour a round cake tin, pour in mixture and bake in a moderate–low oven for 1 hour. Reduce heat to low, put a piece of greased paper on top of the cake and bake for a further 30 minutes.

Christmas Cake

2 cups butter
2 cups soft brown sugar
6 eggs
1 tablespoon treacle
1 small glass brandy
2 tablespoons milk
1 teaspoon mixed spice

1 teaspoon ground cinnamon
4 cups plain flour
1 teaspoon baking powder
2 cups currants
1 1/2 cups sultanas
3/4 cup candied peel
2 cups blanched almonds

Beat butter and sugar to a cream and then add the eggs, one at a time. Stir in the treacle, brandy and milk, followed by the spices, flour and baking powder. Last, mix in the fruits, peel and almonds. Bake in a moderate oven for 3 hours and leave in tin to cool.

'You can keep this cake for quite a long time. Does not get dry. It is a lovely cake.'

ALMOND PASTE FOR CAKES

Sift 1 1/2 cups icing sugar and combine with 4 cups ground almonds. Add 1 egg and beat mixture to a firm paste. Knead for a few minutes and then roll out and cut to shape.

FOR AFTERNOON TEA

For a fashionable afternoon tea the table should be set in the rear of the drawing-room, or, if there are two rooms, in the smaller of them. Coloured cloths are usually used, and the table can be decorated with baskets of flowers and fruit. Do not set the plates, etc., round, but let them be placed in piles of threes and fours here and there, with knives, forks, and spoons where they can be quickly found when required. A few table-napkins beside them (the smaller the napkins the better). The tea equipage should be on a separate table. Wine and cordial should always be on the sideboard; claret cup or champagne cup on the table.
The Antipodean Cookery Book, 1895

CAKES

The recipes that demand 18 eggs, brandy, crushed almonds, and any amount of dried fruit, are scarcely in place in a shilling handbook. The really expensive recipes, as a rule, are for housewives who have no need to enter their kitchens save to play at cooking. Where incomes are anything under £500 a year, the housewife's one desire is towards economy, and she grows excited when she hears of 'Such a nice cake, my dear, and only one egg'. Probably all her life long she has used one egg where recipes demanded two, and omitted the brandy and other expensive items. In one case, a family, whose earliest lesson in economy was, 'Learn to do without things', altered every recipe in a well-known cookery book by the ingenious process of setting an amendment to every dish they fancied. It ran something like this: —

'For butter, read dripping; for every five eggs, use one egg, with baking powder add milk; always omit brandy. Take no notice of suggestions about cream. Divide quantities of fruit by half. Pretend almonds do not exist. Remember that the principal ingredients of a successful family cake are flour, fat, and sugar; and do not be discouraged if other cooks have notions which demand things costing many pence.'

The Melbourne Cookery Book, c. 1900

TEA TRAYS

Tea trays are now generally made oval in form, a great improvement on the old square tray, with rounded corners. They are sold in sets of three, measuring respectively 16, 24 and 30 inches in width. Trays in iron, japanned, cost from 5s to 42s per set, according to finish and ornamentation; and from 25s to 52s 6d in papier mâché. Round waiters for jug stands, card trays, and for use as salvers in bringing in letters, &c., range from 6in. to 12in. in diameter, and from 6d to 3s 9d in price, according to quality.

The Housewife's Treasury of Domestic Information, n.d.

Moist Seed Cake

³/₄ cup butter

³/₄ cup sugar

1 tablespoon caraway seeds

3 eggs, separated

2 cups self-raising flour

1 tablespoon ground almonds

up to ¹/₄ cup milk

Cream the butter and sugar, then stir in the caraway seeds. Beat the egg whites until stiff, then beat the yolks and combine both, mixing well. Add eggs to the butter mixture and stir in the flour and ground almonds. Add enough milk to make a softish mixture. Grease and line a loaf tin and pour in the cake mixture. Bake in a moderate oven for about 1 hour or until a skewer comes out clean. Cool for 15–20 minutes in the tin before turning out.

Shortbread

1 cup butter

¹/₂ cup castor sugar

2 cups plain flour

¹/₄ teaspoon baking powder

pinch of salt

Beat butter and sugar to a cream. Combine the flour, salt and baking powder, then add to the butter mixture, working together well with hands. Roll out the dough until about 6 mm thick, then cut into shapes. Place on ungreased baking sheet, prick each with a fork and bake in a moderate oven for 20–30 minutes or until lightly browned.

'In strawberry season, when you make shortbread, while it is still hot put a layer of strawberries on top, sprinkle with sugar and serve, or roll out the shortbread very thin, spread with strawberries and put a layer of shortbread on top, then cut into squares. Bake and serve hot or cold. Raspberries or mashed peaches may be used instead of strawberries.'

Half a dozen pot and iron holders are not too many in a kitchen; the legs of old tweed and mole-skin trousers make excellent holders. Cut into lengths, pad with any scraps, and then sew across and across in the machine, bind round the edges, and put a loop of tape to hang by.
The Antipodean Cookery Book, 1895

Anzacs (Soldiers' Biscuits)

¹/₂ cup melted butter	1 cup plain flour
2 tablespoons golden syrup	1 cup brown sugar
2 tablespoons water	³/₄ cup desiccated coconut
1 teaspoon bicarbonate of soda	1 cup rolled oats

Melt the butter and golden syrup or treacle with the water in a saucepan. Mix dry ingredients and make a well in the centre. Add soda to butter mixture and pour, boiling, into dry ingredients, stirring well. Place small spoonfuls of the mixture on a greased oven tray, leaving room for spreading, and bake in a slow oven for 10–15 minutes. Leave on tray for a few minutes to harden, then slip onto racks to cool.

Italian Macaroons

3 cups ground almonds	1¹/₂ cups castor sugar
4 egg whites	pinch of salt

Combine ground almonds and sugar. Beat the egg whites with the salt and mix thoroughly with the almond mixture. Spoon onto a greased baking tray, leaving space for the biscuits to spread. Bake in a hot oven for 10–12 minutes, and transfer to a cake rack to cool.

English 'Brown' Scones

3¹/₂ cups wholemeal flour	1 teaspoon salt
2 teaspoons cream of tartar	1 tablespoon melted butter
1 teaspoon bicarbonate of soda	1 tablespoon golden syrup
	2–3 tablespoons milk

Sieve the dry ingredients into a bowl, and add the butter and golden syrup. Mix with enough milk to make a rather soft dough, handling as little as possible. Bake in a hot oven for about 10 minutes.

SOUR MILK
In using sour milk for cooking
be sure to beat it well with the
egg-beater. This will ensure
light muffins, biscuits, or cake.
Do not put carbonate of soda
into the sour milk, but sift it
into flour, as you do baking
powder.
The Hobart Cookery Book, 1900

Buttermilk Scones

4 cups flour

*1 teaspoon bicarbonate of
  soda*

¹/₂ teaspoon cream of tartar

1 level teaspoon salt

1¹/₄ cups buttermilk

Combine the dry ingredients and then work in
buttermilk to form a soft smooth dough. On a floured
board form dough into a round cake about 1 cm thick,
cut into scones, and bake on a floured tin in a hot oven
for about 20 minutes. Serve hot with butter.

VARIATION

Herb Scones: add 1 teaspoon dried mixed herbs with the
dry ingredients.

Pumpkin Scones

2 tablespoons butter

2 tablespoons sugar

*¹/₂ cup cooked mashed
  pumpkin*

¹/₂ cup milk

1 egg, well beaten

2 cups self-raising flour

*2 tablespoons sultanas
  (optional)*

Cream the butter and sugar, then mix in the cold
pumpkin. Gradually add the milk and beaten egg, then
sift in the flour and add the sultanas if used. Mix to a
soft dough using a knife. Turn onto a floured board,
knead for a few seconds, pat out and then cut into
rounds. Place on a greased tray and bake in a hot oven
for 10–15 minutes.

Herb Damper

3 cups self-raising flour
1/4 teaspoon salt
1/3 cup butter
1/2 cup milk or buttermilk
1/2 cup water
6 tablespoons chopped mixed
herbs (parsley, chives,
rosemary)

Sift flour and salt into a bowl and rub in butter until mixture resembles crumbs. Make a well in the centre and lightly mix in milk and water. Last, stir in the herbs. Turn dough onto floured surface, knead lightly and then pat into a round on a greased baking tray. Cut a deepish cross in the top and brush with a little extra milk. Bake for 10 minutes in a hot oven, then reduce heat to moderate and bake for a further 15 minutes. Serve straight from the oven.

Corn Bread

2 cups cornmeal
2 cups plain flour
1 1/2 teaspoons baking powder
pinch of salt
2 tablespoons sugar
1/4 cup melted butter
1 egg
1 cup milk

Place the dry ingredients in a bowl, stirring to mix. Combine the melted butter with the egg and milk, mix well and add gradually to the dry ingredients, stirring constantly. Put mixture in a greased tin and bake in a moderate oven for 20 minutes or until bread is springy and a skewer inserted in the centre comes out clean.

DAMPER
A Bushman's recipe, which some people swear by and others swear at. Make a hole in some flour in a ration bag, pour in a quart pot of boiling water and stir it with a stick until you have a lump of dough, which you lift out from the surrounding flour, slightly flatten and bake in the ashes. A more luxurious way to mix it is to take off your leather legging and mix it on that, or a piece of bark.
The Kookaburra Cookery Book,
1911

BROWNIE, THE SHEARER'S LOAF

Rub ¾lb good dripping into 4lb flour; add 1lb sugar, a pinch each of nutmeg and salt, and currants or raisins as liked. Make a hole in the centre, pour in 1 cup yeast. Have ready some lukewarm water (or milk and water) and make into a soft dough. Then stand aside in a warm place to rise. When sufficiently risen make into loaves and set to rise again; keeping the dough covered and warm. Bake 1 hour or longer if necessary.

Old English Malt Loaf

4 cups wholemeal plain flour
1½ cups sultanas
½ cup soft brown sugar
pinch of salt
1 teaspoon bicarbonate of
  soda

1 tablespoon hot water
1¼ cups milk
½ cup treacle
1 cup malt extract

Sift the flour into a large bowl and stir in the sultanas, sugar and salt. Combine the soda with the hot water and then add the milk. Combine the treacle and malt extract in a small pan and stir until mixture comes to the boil. Pour in milk, mix well, remove from heat and stir into dry ingredients. Mix well, pour into greased and lined loaf tin and bake in a slow oven for 1½–2 hours or until skewer inserted into the middle comes out clean. Cool on a rack and store in an airtight tin.

Walnut Loaf

2 cups self-raising flour
½ cup brown sugar
½ cup finely chopped walnuts
½ teaspoon salt
1 teaspoon baking powder

½ teaspoon mixed spice
1 cup milk
1 egg, beaten
2 tablespoons butter

Mix dry ingredients together, then add the egg and enough milk to form a dough. Butter a loaf tin, pour in mixture and bake in a moderate oven for about 40 minutes.

Nasturtium Sandwiches

Gather some fresh nasturtium flowers and leaves, and drop them into iced water to crisp. Butter slices of bread, spread thickly with cream cheese and then cut into triangles or flower shapes. Place a nasturtium leaf on each slice of bread and top with a layer of petals and a sprinkle of salt before covering with a second slice of bread. Basil leaves may be substituted for the nasturtiums.

Shrimp and Watercress Rolls

1 bunch watercress, washed
 and dried
12 slices bread

½ cup butter
1 × 60 g can shrimp paste

Pick the watercress leaves off the stalks and chop them roughly. Remove the crusts from the bread, roll out each slice with a rolling pin, and then spread with butter. Spread half the bread slices with shrimp paste, and on the others place a layer of chopped cress. Put a cress-covered slice on top of each shrimp slice and roll them up together. Cut each roll in half crosswise.

Potted Fish

250 g shrimps, prawns,
 crayfish or salmon
a pinch each of black pepper,
 ground nutmeg and cayenne

about ¼ cup butter

Remove any bones, scales or skin from the fish, season plentifully with spices, and mash thoroughly or pound in a mortar. Add enough butter to make a smooth paste, then press down well into pots and cover with a layer of clarified butter. Tie them down securely to make airtight.

CRESS
The whole plant abideth green in the winter, and tasteth somewhat hot and sharp.
Culpeper

TOASTED ROLLED
SANDWICHES

Toasted rolled sandwiches may
be spread with any savoury
butter. Minced ingredients
(chicken, ham, oysters, chopped
asparagus, etc.) may be spread
into the butter.

Make rolled sandwiches,
secure with a wooden pick and
brush lightly with butter
outside. Place carefully on a
greased tin plate in hot oven till
light brown and crisp. Remove
picks. Serve at once piled high
on sandwich dish with doyley
under. Garnish with parsley.
*The Schauer Australian Cookery
Book*, 1946

Savoury Butters and Spreads for Sandwiches

GREEN BUTTER

¹/₂ cup butter

*6 anchovy fillets, very finely
  chopped*

2 tablespoons chopped parsley

*2 teaspoons finely chopped
  capers*

*about ¹/₂ cup puréed spinach
  or watercress*

Beat butter to a cream and then add the other
ingredients, using sufficient spinach or cress to colour
the mixture 'nicely'. Season with pepper and salt to
taste.

    This is particularly good with sandwich fillings of
smoked salmon and thinly sliced cucumber, or sardines
mashed with cayenne and a little lemon juice.

ANCHOVY BUTTER

8 anchovy fillets

yolks of 2 hard-boiled eggs

¹/₄ cup butter

pinch of cayenne

squeeze of lemon juice

Mash all the ingredients together until creamy. Keep in
a closed jar and use for sandwiches or for croutons or
savoury toasts.

CHEESE PASTE

1 cup grated tasty cheese

1 teaspoon dry mustard

2–4 tablespoons butter

pinch of cayenne or nutmeg

*¹/₂ teaspoon Madeira
  (optional)*

Work the cheese into the butter until creamy. Flavour
with the mustard and cayenne or nutmeg, and Madeira
if used.

CHUTNEY AND EGG

3 hard-boiled eggs

1 tablespoon chutney

pepper and salt to taste

Fork the egg yolks and whites into crumbs. Butter the
bread, spread with the chutney and then top with a
generous layer of the eggs. Season to taste.

MUSHROOM FILLING

1 cup chopped mushrooms   *salt to taste*
2 teaspoons butter
pinch each of cayenne and
  ground coriander

Fry the chopped mushrooms briskly in the butter over a medium heat so that they do not exude too much liquid. Season with cayenne, coriander and salt to taste. Sandwich between thinly sliced brown bread and butter.

VARIOUS MEAT FILLINGS

- minced ham or roast beef spread thinly with horseradish or mustard
- minced ham, a little mayonnaise and a few chopped pickles
- liverwurst with Green Butter (page 144)
- thinly sliced roast lamb or mutton spread with mint butter
- minced roast duck mixed with a little orange juice and grated orange peel

HOW TO INCREASE BUTTER

This can be eaten with bread, sandwiches or hot scones, etc., but cannot be used in cooking. Soak 1 tablespoonful gelatine in a cup of milk till soft. Heat in a small pan, then remove from heat and shred in 1 cup butter and stir till melted. Add half a teaspoon salt and stir till all the milk is worked into the butter. It will appear to curdle, but will gradually all be absorbed. Put aside in a cool place to harden.

Jams, Jellies and Other Preserves

AS JAMES COOK had reported that New South Wales lacked native fruit, the First Fleet brought with it huge stocks of European varieties. These were quickly planted at Farm Cove, which is now part of the Sydney Botanic Gardens, where the original rectangular fruit and vegetable plots can still be seen. The first free settlers often brought cuttings of their favourite cherry or plum or gooseberry with them; as water was strictly rationed on board ship, they kept the shoots alive by embedding them in raw potatoes. Most grew at a great rate in our warm climate and nearly every cottage had its fruit trees and berries, which amazed people by their abundant crops. The proud owners made innumerable jams and jellies, which stood in glistening rows in the pantries that graced even the humbler cottages. Chutneys and fruit pickles were also very popular as a means of enlivening dull meats or as an accompaniment to 'colonial curries'.

In their longing to have fruit available throughout the year our forebears often made attempts at drying some of the surplus from each harvest, but with very uncertain results. Preserving fruit – indeed, meats and even milk – in bottles became much more widespread with the introduction of 'Fowler's Vacuum Pasteurising Preserving Process' early this century. With factories in Sydney and Melbourne turning out Fowler jars by the thousand, and with countless shops supplying them, housewives all over Australia learnt to bottle, and stewed fruit and fruit pies were found on tables for every Sunday dinner, whatever the season.

Today the availability of commercial spreads and preserves has led to a decline in home preserving, even in the bush. Yet many busy cooks still take an atavistic pleasure in overseeing a simmering pan of aromatic fruits destined for the larder.

ABOUT PRESERVING
Jam-making is almost an art in itself, apart from general cookery. And you frequently find a lady who is no cook as regards culinary matters in general particularly clever at all sorts of preserving. I think everything depends upon the eye—a quickness in seeing when the preserve is done. There are some people who are always undecided, and will call in every member of the household to say if they think it is cooked enough; while others seem to know instinctively when to take the pan off.
The Antipodean Cookery Book, 1895

Brandied Peach Jam

1 kg peaches, peeled and
  pitted
1 cup water
juice and rind of 1 lemon

3 cups sugar
1 cinnamon stick
2–3 tablespoons brandy

Put the peaches in a large pan with the water and simmer, covered, until tender. Add lemon juice, sugar and cinnamon stick, stirring until sugar is dissolved. Bring to the boil and cook until setting point is reached. Remove cinnamon stick, stir in the brandy and pour into hot jars. Allow to cool before sealing.

VARIATION

Peach and Passionfruit Jam: add the pulp of 3 passionfruit with the sugar.

Easy Orange Marmalade

1 kg oranges
2 lemons
9 cups water

8 cups sugar
1/2 cup whisky (optional)

Slice the oranges and lemons as thinly as possible and place in large pot. Cover with the water and leave to stand for 24 hours. Bring to the boil, add the sugar and then remove from heat and stir until sugar is dissolved. Leave for a further 24 hours. The next day simmer for 2 hours, until the fruit rind is transparent, then boil for 30 minutes until the marmalade sets when tested.

For Whisky Marmalade, add the whisky just before the end of the cooking time.

Blackberry and Apple Jam

2 green apples, peeled and
  sliced
1 kg blackberries (or
  blueberries)

2 cups sugar
1/2 cup water
juice of 1 lemon

Put the apples, blackberries and water in a pan and
simmer until mushy. Add the lemon juice and sugar,
and boil for about 15 minutes or until jam sets when
tested.

Fig and Ginger Jam

1 kg figs
3 cups sugar
1/2 cup vinegar
3 tablespoons finely chopped
  crystallised ginger

juice and grated rind of
  1 lemon

Cut figs into four, place in a large bowl and cover with
the sugar. Leave overnight. The next day place the figs
and liquid in a pot and add the vinegar, ginger, and
lemon juice and rind. Simmer for about 30 minutes or
until mixture sets when tested. Pour into hot jars and
seal when cool.

Apricot and Almond Jam

1 kg dried apricots
1.5 litres water
1 kg sugar
juice of 1 lemon

1/2 teaspoon salt
3/4 cup blanched almonds,
  halved

Cover the apricots with the water and soak overnight.
Boil for 15 minutes, then add sugar, lemon juice and
salt, and boil for a further 30 minutes. Add almonds at
the end of the cooking time.

BANANA JAM

This very wholesome fruit
makes an excellent jam. Choose
sound bananas, peel, slice and
weigh them, allowing three-
quarters of a pint of orange
juice, the juice of one lemon,
and about half a pound of sugar
to every pound of fruit. Now
put the bananas and juices
together in a stone jar, which,
in turn, should stand in a pan
of water. There is no water,
remember, with the fruit, which
must be allowed to come gently
to the boil. When it boils, stir in
the sugar, and let it boil till it
thickens, meanwhile removing
all scum and stirring constantly
with a wooden spoon. In about
15 minutes it should be ready to
pour into jars. Allow to cool
before sealing down.

A NEW SOUTH WALES GARDEN

The garden hedge is of lemon; laid, and trimmed like a holly hedge. On each side the middle walk, and fronting the visitor as he enters, is a mass of plantain stems (here called the banana) full thirty feet in circumference, and, in the season, laden with fruit. The stems are about twelve feet in height; and from them depend the beautiful purple sheaths of the younger fruit. There are many plots of them about the garden; and a bunch of the fruit sells in Sydney for half-a-crown. On the sides of some of the walks are orange, lemon, and shaddock trees, the citron, and the flowering almond; and, on the sides of others, standard peaches and apricots, and weeping nectarines, with occasionally mulberries, and the finest varieties of pears. The squares are filled with plum, apple, cherry, and medlar trees. There are two very fine walnut-trees, being amongst the first that have borne in the colony. Other squares between the walks, to the extent of three acres, are filled with vines in full bearing.

Joseph Phipps Townsend, 1848

JELLIES

A special saucepan should be kept for jellies, and used for nothing else. For a strainer take an ordinary kitchen tea-cloth. Jelly bags are very troublesome things. They soon harden, and are difficult to keep clean. On the other hand, a teacloth is easily washed, and yet it makes a most effectual strainer. If no jelly stand is at hand, turn a chair upside down on the table, and tie a cloth firmly over the legs. When the jelly is ready to strain, pour some boiling water through the cloth, and have two basins ready that will slip easily through the rails of the chair. When the jelly is all in the cloth remove the first basin and place the other one, and pour what ran through the strainer back into the cloth, as that will not be quite clear. It is only necessary to strain the jelly once; but do not hurry it—let it drop through in its own time.

The Kingswood Cookery Book, n.d.

Orange Butter

juice and rind of 6 oranges
1½ cups sugar
1½ cups butter
4 egg yolks

Melt butter in a pan with the sugar, and orange rind and juice. Allow to cool a little, combine with the beaten egg yolks and stir mixture over boiling water until it thickens. When cool, put into pots and cover.

Herb Jelly with Sherry

2 cups white-wine vinegar
⅓ cup dry sherry
½ cup sugar
1 cup chopped fresh herbs,
  firmly packed
2 tablespoons gelatine

Put the vinegar, sherry and sugar in a pan and stir until the sugar dissolves. Pour over the chopped herbs and set aside to cool just a little. Stir in the gelatine until dissolved and pour mixture into sterilised jars (keep stirring as it begins to set, to distribute the herbs evenly).

Pickled Pears

1 cinnamon stick
4 cloves
6 cups sugar
1 litre vinegar
3 kg unripe pears, peeled

Tie the cinnamon stick and cloves in muslin. Place in the pan with the sugar and vinegar, bring to the boil and remove from heat. Put the pears into a pan, cover with water and simmer gently for 1 hour. Drain the pears, place in spiced vinegar and then simmer until quite tender (up to 1 hour). Remove with a slotted spoon and pack into jars. Boil syrup until thick, pour over pears, and seal.

ON IMPORTED PRESERVES
The British-made fruit, jams and jellies, lose their fine flavour in crossing the Line to the Colonies, and become hard and tasteless. The Tasmania jams have acquired a repute in the Colonies for their goodness and fine aroma, and the demand for them is very great.
The English and Australian Cookery Book, 1864

THE COLONEL'S
MUSHROOM KETCHUP
Break 6 lb of mushrooms into
an earthenware vessel, sprinkle
them with ¼ lb salt. Put the
vessel containing the
mushrooms into a cool oven for
about 12 hours. Then strain and
measure the juice and boil for
quarter of an hour. Add for
each quart of juice a ¼ oz
allspice, ½ oz ginger, 2 blades
mace, 1 oz pepper. Let all boil
quickly for half an hour, strain,
let cool before bottling. Cork
well and seal corks.

Modern Mushroom Ketchup

750 g mushrooms, quartered
½ cup brown sugar
2½ cups vinegar
1 onion, finely chopped

2 teaspoons ground allspice
2 teaspoons ground ginger
1 tablespoon salt
¼ teaspoon ground pepper

Put everything into a large pan and bring to the boil,
stirring until the sugar dissolves. Cover the pan and
simmer for 30 minutes, or until mushrooms are soft.
Purée in a blender, return to pan and simmer for 5
minutes. Pour into hot jars and seal at once.

Traditional Tomato Sauce

2 kg tomatoes, chopped
2 onions, chopped
4 cloves garlic, chopped
½ teaspoon cayenne
1 teaspoon peppercorns

1 teaspoon allspice berries
6 cloves
2½ cups vinegar
¾ cup sugar
1 teaspoon salt

Put the tomatoes and onions in a large pan with the
spices (tie the whole spices in a muslin bag). Simmer
until the vegetables are tender (about 30 minutes), then
remove muslin bag and purée contents of pan in a
blender. Return to pan, add vinegar, sugar and salt, and
bring to the boil. Simmer for about 1 hour, stirring from
time to time, and then pour into hot, sterilised bottles.
Seal while still hot.

FOWLER'S PATENT APPLIANCES

Sergeant-Major George Fowler, of the Maidstone Medical Staff Corps of the British Army, was, as his photographs reveal, 'a fine figure of a man'. He served in the army for thirty years and won a Silver Medal for Meritorious Service, but his real achievements were the improvements he made to the diet of wounded soldiers in some of the hot and barren lands where some of the British Army's campaigns were fought. First he invented a camp stove where light hot meals could be cooked for the sick and convalescent, and then he perfected his vacuum preserving process, which enabled fresh fruit from home to enhance the men's diet and no doubt saved many lives. His sons carried on this work and introduced his bottling methods to Australia and many other countries:

The Fruit Bottling industry, both in the home and commercially has been, by means of my Patented Appliances and system, increased enormously since I first placed them on the market at Maidstone, Kent, 1899.

Annually, during recent years, more than a million bottles of Fruits, Vegetables, Mushrooms, Game, etc., etc., are successfully preserved with my Patented Appliances and by the instructions given in this Book.

Many Fruiterers, Grocers, Dairymen, Farmers and others, have, by using my Patented Appliances, added the Bottling industry to their business, and by doing so turned what was waste and loss into profit.

I take this opportunity of thanking my numerous patrons for recommending my Patents and System of Preserving Foods, Fruits, etc., and I hope to be favoured with a continuance of their esteemed orders.

How to Bottle, 1940

Spiced Plums

1.5 kg ripe red or black plums
2 sticks cinnamon
6 cloves

1 litre vinegar
2 cups sugar

Prick the plums all over and put into jars with 'a scrap' of cinnamon and 2 cloves to each jar. Boil the vinegar and sugar together for about 5 minutes, or until syrupy, then pour over the plums. Leave until cold before sealing.

Mango Chutney

1 kg mangoes, peeled and
  chopped
750 g raisins
750 g dates, chopped
3 onions, chopped
4 cloves garlic, finely chopped
1/2 cup green ginger, finely
  chopped

1/3 cup mustard seed
1 cup brown sugar
3–4 red chillies, seeded and
  chopped
2 tablespoons salt
1 litre vinegar

Slice half the mangoes and purée the other half. Do the same with raisins and dates. Put all the ingredients into a large pan and boil until soft and pulpy (about 1 hour). Pour into jars and seal when cold.

'An Indian recipe, and one that I have used for many years and can vouch for its excellence.'

PRESERVED PAWPAW
Peel three large pawpaws (not too ripe), take out seeds, cut in slices. Put in boiling water for 1/2 hour, then drain in a clean cloth. Dissolve 2 lb sugar in 1 quart water, add the pawpaw, cook carefully 1 hour. Take pan off fire, stand till next day in the syrup, then put pan on cool part of stove, cook gently till syrup is thick. Take fruit out of syrup, drain, sprinkle with crystal sugar, put in sun to dry. It will take about a week to dry, and must be turned every day and placed on dry dishes.

To Preserve Husbands
Husbands, like peaches, will not keep the year round unless they are well preserved. First select him carefully; be sure he is not too green, neither should he be over-ripe . . . Husbands grown in the tropics of pleasure look very fine, but are usually insipid. The homegrown are best. Select your husband, if possible, from a family tree, growing on the sunny side of a church. You will be sure then that he is sound at heart. Unsound husbands, like unsound peaches, often have to be sorrowfully cast away . . . Your preserving pan (the home) must be neat and clean. Husbands, like peaches, look very black if this is untidy. Give him plenty of sweetness—much sugar is needed—vinegar is never used in sweet preserves. If you think he demands a little spice, use it with caution. Do not keep stirring him up, neither should you keep poking him with sharp points to see if he is done—it will spoil his looks. If you follow the above recipe, love will be well preserved.
The Green and Gold Cookery Book, c. 1928

Rich Pumpkin Chutney

1 kg pumpkin, peeled and sliced into 1-cm-thick rectangles
2 cups peeled and sliced tomatoes
1 cup sliced onions
2 cloves garlic, sliced
¹⁄₃ cup sultanas
2 cups soft brown sugar
1 tablespoon salt
2 teaspoons ground ginger
1 teaspoon ground black pepper
1 teaspoon ground allspice
3 cups red-wine or cider vinegar

Put everything into a large pan and bring gently to the boil. Simmer until mixture thickens, stirring frequently to prevent sticking. Pour into jars and seal when cold.

Pickled Onions

1 kg pickling onions
¹⁄₂ cup salt
2 cups wine vinegar
¹⁄₃ cup sugar
1 tablespoon pickling spice
extra 1 teaspoon salt

Put the unpeeled onions in a bowl and cover with boiling water. Leave to steep for 20 minutes. Drain, peel and replace in bowl. Cover with fresh water and the ¹⁄₂ cup of salt, and leave, covered, at least overnight (preferably for 48 hours). Drain and rinse. Place the remaining ingredients in a pan and bring to the boil. Pack onions into sterilised jars and pour boiling vinegar over. Seal, and store in a cool place for a few weeks before using.

Chilli Vinegar

12 small red chillies   *2½ cups vinegar*

Slit the chillies and put into the vinegar. Leave for 10 days, shaking occasionally, then strain and bottle.

Lemon or Lime Pickle

10 medium lemons or limes, sliced

2 teaspoons rock salt

1 cup oil

4 fresh birdseye chillies, seeded and chopped

1 teaspoon yellow mustard seeds

1 teaspoon fenugreek seeds

1 tablespoon grated fresh ginger

6 cloves garlic, finely chopped

2 cups wine vinegar

Layer lemons or limes with the salt in a large bowl and leave overnight. Rinse and drain. Heat oil in a large pot and add the chillies, mustard, fenugreek, ginger and garlic. Stir over a medium heat for a few minutes, then combine with the limes and vinegar. Pack into sterilised jars and seal when cold. Leave for at least a week before using.

CUMQUATS IN GIN

Wipe two dozen cumquats and prick all over with a fine skewer. Layer into a tall jar with a bottle of gin and 3 cups of sugar. Cover tightly, turning occasionally for the first few days, until the sugar has dissolved. This is best left for 6 months before use.

LIQUEUR BLACK CURRANT

To 8 quarts of black currants put 4 quarts of gin, bruise them and let it stand 24 hours. Then strain it through a jelly bag, to every quart of juice put 1 lb of loaf sugar. Bottle and cork it well. This is a delicious liqueur and will keep for years.

HERB ESSENCE

Put 1 penny bunch each thyme, sage and marjoram with 1 pint water and boil very slowly to extract all the flavour. When reduced to half a pint add 1 pint good white vinegar and boil a few minutes longer, adding salt and pepper. Remove from the fire, and when cold strain and bottle, adding a large spoonful of whisky last of all as a preservative. One tea or tablespoon, according to size, will flavour a stew, hash or mince.

Whisky Apples

450 g apples, peeled and
  cored but left whole
1¹/₂ cups sugar
juice and thinly pared rind of
  1 lemon
¹/₄ teaspoon ground ginger
¹/₄ teaspoon ground
  cinnamon
¹/₄ teaspoon vanilla essence
¹/₄ cup whisky

Put the apples in a pan with the other ingredients and
simmer slowly for 1 hour, turning gently once or twice.
When they are transparent, take out carefully with a
slotted spoon and put in wide-mouthed jars. Boil the
liquid for 5 minutes until syrupy and then pour over
apples. Seal tightly while still hot.

Candied Peel

2 oranges (or 4 lemons or
  1 grapefruit)
1 cup water
¹/₂ cup sugar
extra sugar

Peel the fruit and cut peel into strips. Place in a pan
with half the water, bring to the boil and simmer for 5
minutes. Drain thoroughly. Now put rest of water and
the sugar into a pan, bring to the boil and simmer for 5
minutes until sugar dissolves. Add the peel and cook
gently, without stirring, until syrup is absorbed. Sprinkle
extra sugar onto a plate and place peel on it in a single
layer. Sprinkle more sugar over the top, turn peel until
well coated and then set aside to dry. Store in an airtight
container.

GLYCERINE AND
LIME JUICE
(For Sunburn and after
Motoring)
2 ozs of sweet oil of almonds;
2 ozs of lime water; 1 teaspoon
of glycerine; a few drops oil of
lemon to scent. Put all together
in a bottle and shake well.
Apply to face and hands, if
sunburnt leave on 10 minutes,
wipe off and powder with
Fuller's Earth.
The Kookaburra Cookery Book,
1911

GLOSSARY OF OLD COOKING TERMS

Au maigre	A dish prepared without meat, especially during Lent.
Brose	A Scottish dish originally prepared by cooking oatmeal in water. For Athol Brose, a popular cold cure, whisky toddy was stirred into the mixture, the whole being strained and only the liquid served.
Carmine	Another name for cochineal, the red food colouring.
Chaudfroid	A dish of cold, cooked meat served in a jelly or sauce.
Diable/Devil	A sharp, hot seasoned dish.
Dripping	Fat melted from a roast, formerly saved and much used for cooking or as a spread.
Entrée	Originally this referred to hot or cold *side* dishes rather than the course preceding the main dish.
Entremet	A second course, usually consisting of dressed vegetables or a sweet dish.
Hash	A type of stew, comprising chopped meat and vegetables which have already been cooked. Derived from the French *hacher*, to chop into small pieces.
Ketchup	A spicy vinegar-based sauce or relish.
Liebig	A brand of meat concentrates or soups, named after a German chemist, Justus, Baron von Liebig.
Lard	White pork fat which has been melted down and purified. 'It is to be feared that Lard is subject to extensive adulterations'.
Maizena	A fine flour prepared from maize, 'Indian corn'.
Mask	To cover or coat, e.g. with a thick sauce.
Noyau	A brandy-based liqueur flavoured with almond or other fruit kernels.
Peck	A dry measure equal to 2 gallons or 9 litres.
Pluck	The lungs, liver and heart of an animal.
Porter	A dark-brown, bitter beer (not to be confused with port).
Prunella	A preparation of fused nitre or saltpetre, chiefly used to treat throat infections.
Raspings	Grated ('rasped') breadcrumbs.
Ratafia	A liqueur flavoured with almonds or other fruit kernels.
Remove	One of the dishes making up a meal, especially joints of meat.
Saltpetre	Potassium nitrate: a white salty substance used in preserving meat.
Tamis/Tammy	A fine cloth such as muslin, used to strain soups, sauces, etc.

$\mathscr{S}$ELECTED REFERENCES

Books

Advice to a Young Lady in the Colonies (being a letter sent from Mrs E. of England to Maria Macarthur in the Colony of New South Wales in 1812), Melbourne, 1979

'An Australian Aristologist' (Edward Abbott), *The English and Australian Cookery Book*, London, 1864

Beeton, Mrs Isabella, *The Book of Household Management*, London, 1861

——, *The Housewife's Treasury of Domestic Information*, London, no date

Colcord, Mrs Anna, *A Friend in the Kitchen*, Melbourne, 1918

W. H. Comstock Co. Ltd (proprietors of Dr Morse's Indian Root Pills), *Valuable Cookery Suggestions*, Sydney, no date (1920s?)

Cooper, Charles, *The English Table in Literature and History*, London, no date (1930s?)

Corrie, Mrs Sophie, *The Art of Canning, Bottling and Preserving Fruit*, Sydney, 1909

Drake, Miss, *Every Lady's Cookery Book*, Melbourne, no date

Drummond, Sir Jack, *The Englishman's Food*, London, no date

Elmes, F. F., *The Melbourne Cookery Book*, Melbourne, no date (c. 1900)

Fahey, Warren, *When Mabel Laid the Table*, State Library of NSW, 1992

Fletcher, Nora, *500 6d Recipes*, London, 1934

Fowler, Sgt-Major Geo., *How to Bottle Fruit, Vegetables, Game, Rabbits, Poultry, Meat, Milk etc.*, Reading, abridged ed., 1940

Futter, Emily, *Miss Futter's Australian Home Cookery*, 4th ed., Sydney, 1916

Garrett, Theodore F., *The Encyclopedia of Practical Cookery*, London, no date (c. 1900)

Good Things Made, Said and Done in Every Home and Household, Leeds, 1885

Hackett, Lady (ed.), *The Australian Household Guide*, Perth, 1916

Helping Hands: the Blackies' Domestic Economy Reader No. 6, London (inscribed 1899)

Hobart Gas Company, *The Household Gas Cookery Book*, London, no date

The Home Golden Cookery Book, Bendigo, no date

Hooper, Dr Mary, *Nelson's Home Comforts*, London, 1884

The Kandy Koola Cookery Book and Housewife's Companion, for Presentation to the Ladies of Victoria, 1898

The Kingswood Cookery Book, Melbourne, no date

The Lady Victoria Buxton Girls' Club, Adelaide, *The Kookaburra Cookery Book*, Melbourne, no date

Landmarks of Australian Gastronomy, University of NSW, 1988

Maclurcan, Mrs, *Mrs Maclurcan's Cookery Book*, Sydney?, 1898

Marshall, A. B., *The Book of Ices*, London, 4th ed., no date (c. 1880)

Methodist Central Mission, *The Hobart Cookery Book*, Hobart, 1900

Moffat, Mrs Willie, *The Berrambool Receipt Book*, Melbourne, 1915

Monro, Miss Amie M., *The Practical Australian Cookery*, Sydney, 4th ed., 1913

Moore, J. V., *The Housewife's Friend?*, Brisbane, 1908

Pell, Flora, *Our Cookery Book*, Melbourne, no date

Pyke, Lillian M., *Australian Etiquette*, Melbourne, rev. ed., 1960

Raffald, Mrs Elizabeth, *The Experienced English Housekeeper*, London, 1769

Rawson, Mrs Lance, *The Queensland Cookery Book*, Maryborough, 1878

——, *An Australian Enquiry Book*, Melbourne, 1894

——, *The Antipodean Cookery Book and Kitchen Companion*, Rockhampton, 1895

——, 'Reminiscences', *The Queenslander*, 1920

Ross, Isabel, *Cookery Class Recipes*, Melbourne, 1900

Rutledge, Mrs Forster, *The Goulburn Cookery Book*, Sydney, 1899

The Schauer Australian Cookery Book, Brisbane, 9th ed., 1946

Shaw, Mrs Wharton, *600 Tested Recipes*, Melbourne, 1908

Story, F. Fawcett, *Australian Economic Cookery Book and Housewife's Companion*, Sydney, 1900

Symons, Michael, *One Continuous Picnic*, Adelaide, 1982

Ulrich, Laura L., *Good Food: How to Prepare It*, Warburton, 1912

Western Australia Education Department, *The Golden Wattle Cookery Book*, Melbourne, no date

Winning, Mrs Theo, *The Household Manual*, Sydney, 1898

Women's Christian Temperance Union, *Tested Recipes*, Bendigo, 1900

Women's Missionary Association of the Presbyterian Church of N.S.W., *Cookery Book of Good and Tried Recipes*, Sydney, 1895

Women's Missionary Union, Queensland Presbyterian Missions, *W.M.U. Cookery Book*, c. 1894

Wood, Beverley, *Tucker in Australia*, Melbourne, 1977

Yates, Lucy, *In Camp and Kitchen: A Handy Guide to Emigrants and Settlers*, London, 1912

Manuscripts

Hanmer, Marg¹, untitled, September Ye '22, 1780

Margaret Tyseyman's Book, 1842

Mary Mitchell's Receipts Book, Barfold, Victoria, no date (born 1845)

Anonymous, untitled, 1875

Emily Bearpark, untitled, 1870s

S. J. Williams, untitled, Castlemaine, c. 1900

$\mathcal{C}$ONVERSION TABLES

These measures are approximate only.

Solid Measures*

Imperial	Metric	Standard
1 oz	25 g	1 tablespoon
2 oz	50 g	¼ cup
4 oz	125 g	½ cup
8 oz (½ lb)	225 g	1 cup
16 oz (1 lb)	450 g	2 cups
2¼ lb	1 kg	4½ cups

Liquid Measures

Imperial	Metric	Standard
¼ pint (1 gill)	125 ml	½ cup
½ pint	300 ml	1¼ cups
—	500 ml	2 cups
1¾ pints	1 litre	4 cups
1 quart	1.2 litres	4½ cups
8 pints (1 gallon)	4 litres	—

* Measures vary for some fine ingredients. With grated cheese, soft breadcrumbs, and flour, for example, 1 oz/25 g = ¼ cup and 8 oz/250 g = 2 cups.

Oven Temperatures

	Electric		Gas	
	°C	°F	°C	°F
Low or warm	150	300	150–160	300–325
Moderate–low	160	325	160–175	325–350
Moderate	175	350	175–190	350–375
Moderate–hot	190	375	190–205	375–400
Hot	205	400	205–230	400–450
Very hot	230	450	230–260	450–500

$\mathcal{I}$ N D E X